COUNTRIES IN OUR WORLD

USA

Lisa Klobuchar

W

FRANKLIN WATTS

LONDON • SYDNEY

First published in 2010 by
Franklin Watts
338 Euston Road
London NW1 3BH

Franklin Watts Australia
Level 17/207 Kent Street
Sydney NSW 2000

Produced for Franklin Watts by
White-Thomson Publishing Ltd
+44 (0) 843 208 7460
www.wtpub.co.uk

Series consultant: Rob Bowden
Editor: Sonya Newland
Designer: Clare Nicholas
Picture researcher: Amy Sparks

A CIP catalogue record for this book is available
from the British Library.

Dewey Classification: 973.9'32

ISBN 978 0 7496 9204 9

Printed in Malaysia

Franklin Watts is a division of Hachette Children's
Books, an Hachette UK company

www.hachette.co.uk

Picture Credits
Corbis: 7 (Andrew Gombert/epa), 13 (Bettmann), 14
(Ed Kashi), 15 (Ed Kashi), 16 (Jeff Zelevansky/Reuters),
17 (John Gress/Reuters), 20 (Reuters), 23 (Steven
Georges/Press-Telegram), 25 (Matthew Cavanaugh/
epa), 28 (Guy Reynolds/Dallas Morning News).
Dreamstime: 4-5 (Michele Perbellini), 8 (Aliaksandr
Nikitsin), 9 (Ben Renard-Wiart), 10 (Elimitchell),
18–19 (Dreamshot); **FEMA News Photo:** 26 (Andrea
Booher); **iStock:** 29 (Jani Bryson); **NASA:** 21;
Shutterstock: 1 (Albert de Bruijn), 11 (Andy Z), 12
(Matt McClain), 19 (Byron W. Moore), 22 (Gary718),
24 (Albert de Bruijn), 27 (Christopher Halloran);
US Department of Defense: 6 (Edwin I Wriston).

Contents

Introducing the USA

Its wealth and military might make the United States of America the most powerful country in the world. Despite criticism by other countries over economic problems and unpopular wars fought in Afghanistan and Iraq, the USA still has a major influence on international economics and politics.

Where in the world?

Most of the USA lies in the middle part of the continent of North America. This is where 48 of the nation's 50 states are located. Two other states lie far away. Alaska is beyond the north-west border of Canada, the country to the north of the USA. Hawaii is made up of several islands in the South Pacific Ocean. Beyond the southernmost states lie Central and South America.

◀ *The Statue of Liberty is a symbol of the freedom that is one of the most treasured American values.*

IT'S A FACT!

The Statue of Liberty commemorates the signing of the Declaration of Independence in 1776, when America began a campaign against British rule. The 46-m (150-ft) statue (a gift from France) stands at the entrance to New York Harbor, welcoming ships to 'the land of the free'.

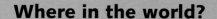

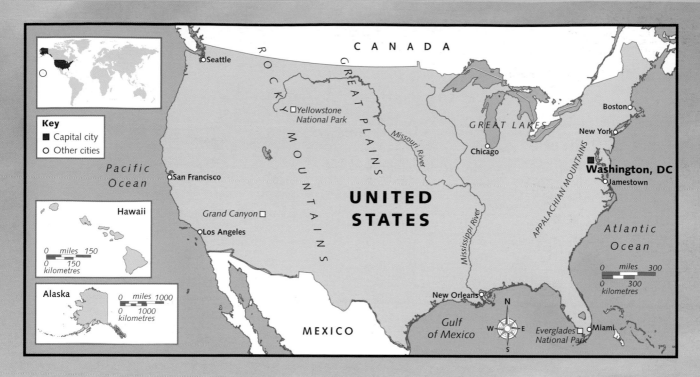

Key
■ Capital city
○ Other cities

▲ *The USA, the world's third-largest country, shares borders with Canada in the north and Mexico in the south.*

A young nation

The USA was one of the first nations created when people moved away from their native countries and formed colonies overseas. About 400 years ago, people from Great Britain travelled across the ocean and first settled on the east coast of what is now the USA. In 1776, these settlers declared their independence from Britain, and after an eight-year war the USA officially became an independent country.

A nation of immigrants

Throughout its history, the USA has attracted settlers from all over the world. People moved there to seek freedoms and opportunities they did not have in their own countries, and its many immigrant communities have all left their stamp on American life.

Global superpower

After the collapse of the USSR in the 1990s, the USA emerged as the only superpower in the world. But what makes it so powerful? For one thing, it is the richest country in the world. The value of US goods and services is almost twice that of China, the world's second largest economy.

Military strength

The USA also has the mightiest military in the world. It spends about 10 times more on its armed forces than China and Russia, which rank second and third. Despite this, China continues to grow in global power and influence, and will probably challenge the USA's status as the only superpower.

BASIC DATA

Official name: **United States of America**

Capital: **Washington, D.C.**

Size: **9,826,630 sq km (3,794,083 sq miles)**

Population: **307,212,123**

Currency: **Dollar**

▼ *Although the war in Iraq is over, there is still a strong US military presence there.*

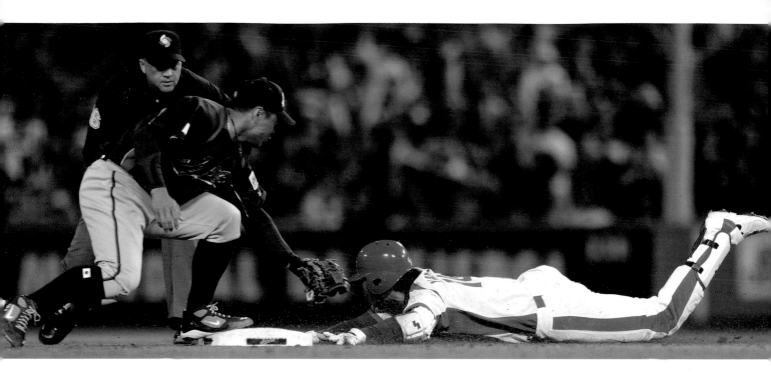

Troubled times

The USA started a war in Iraq in 2003, believing that the Iraqis were hiding powerful weapons known as 'weapons of mass destruction'. The war itself lasted only a few weeks, but by 2009 about 140,000 American troops remained in Iraq. Although countries such as the UK supported the invasion of Iraq, others disagreed and many Americans protested against it, too. In 2008, poor investments caused some important financial companies in the USA to fail. Many other countries were affected as a result, and a worldwide recession began.

▲ *Japan and South Korea play in the final of the 2009 World Baseball Classic. American sports like this are enjoyed all over the world.*

Cultural leader

One major way the USA makes its mark on the rest of the world is through its culture. American fast-food chains such as McDonalds and Pizza Hut thrive in many countries. American sports such as baseball and basketball have become popular throughout the world. People all over the globe enjoy and copy American music, art, fashion, film and television. However, not everyone appreciates the USA's influence on their countries' arts and culture, feeling that their own are lost as America's influence spreads.

The USA covers the entire middle section of the continent of North America. It is the world's third largest country – only Russia and Canada are larger. The USA stretches from the Pacific Ocean in the west to the Atlantic Ocean in the east. It shares a long border with Canada in the north and with Mexico in the south.

East of the Mississippi

The Mississippi River forms a dividing line between the different landscapes of the USA. East of the Mississippi lie the temperate forests of the Midwest and Northeast regions. In the far eastern part of the country is a region of highlands with several forested mountain ranges. The land slopes down to the east coast, which has many sandy beaches.

▼ *With a surface area of 82,413 sq km (31,820 sq miles), Lake Superior is a major waterway for transport of goods, as well as a destination for tourists.*

THE HOME OF...

The Great Lakes

The Great Lakes – five large, freshwater lakes on the border with Canada in the north-central part of the USA – contain about 20 per cent of the world's fresh water. The largest of the Great Lakes, Lake Superior, is the largest freshwater lake in the world.

West of the Mississippi

A huge, flat region lies in the middle part of the country. Part of this region is called the Great Plains, a fairly dry grassland where few trees grow. The towering Rocky Mountains run from Alaska to Mexico. To the west of the Rockies is a region of deserts, dry lowlands and high plateaus. Mountain ranges and wide valleys make up the far western part of the country.

Climate

Most of the USA is in the Earth's temperate middle latitudes. This means that it has cool or cold winters and warm or hot summers. But the country has many different climates. Scorching deserts lie in the south-west. In the north-west are cool, green temperate rainforests. Alaska has an arctic climate, with bitterly cold winters and short, cool summers. Hawaii and Florida have a tropical climate, with warm temperatures all year round.

▼ *South-western USA is hot and dry. Here, in the desert of Utah, the wind has worn the sandstone into shapes such as pillars and arches.*

IT'S A FACT!

Hurricane Katrina struck the Gulf Coast of the USA in August 2005, destroying parts of the historic city of New Orleans in Louisiana, as well as damaging other coastal cities in Mississippi and Alabama. About 1,300 people died as a result of the storm, and it caused an estimated $125 billion in damage. In terms of economic damage, Katrina was the worst natural disaster in US history.

Protecting wildlife

The USA has hundreds of national parks and refuges, where the environment is conserved and wildlife protected. The largest refuge is the 81,000 sq km (31,250 sq mile) Yukon Delta National Wildlife Refuge in Alaska. In 2002 and 2003, President George W. Bush tried to pass laws that would allow oil companies to drill in the Alaskan Arctic National Wildlife Refuge. Many people were afraid of the damage this would do to the environment. The refuge is home to grizzly bears, caribou and polar bears, as well as many types of birds and fish. In the end the laws were not passed.

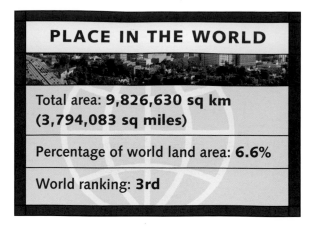

PLACE IN THE WORLD

Total area: **9,826,630 sq km (3,794,083 sq miles)**	
Percentage of world land area: **6.6%**	
World ranking: **3rd**	

▼ *Animals such as caribou (reindeer) and moose make their homes in freezing Alaska. The country's largest national parks lie in this relatively unpopulated area.*

▲ *In some big cities, such as Los Angeles, air pollution is so bad that a permanent smog hangs over them.*

Controlling pollution

The USA faces many environmental challenges. Pollution from factories, power plants, farms and cars endangers people's health and the natural environment. The USA sets pollution rules through the Environmental Protection Agency (EPA), but it is still the world's worst polluter and the biggest generator of waste. To tackle this problem, the US government has passed laws to control pollution, such as the Clean Air Act and the Clean Water Act.

IT STARTED HERE

Earth Day

Earth Day is a special day to make people aware of the environmental issues threatening our planet. It was first celebrated in the USA on 22 April 1970, after Senator Gaylord Nelson decided to organize a protest at how little was being done to protect the environment. Earth Day is now celebrated all over the world every year.

Many people call the USA a 'melting pot'. This means that people from all over the world have settled there and brought their unique traditions and beliefs, which have all influenced American culture today.

Colonial life

The first people to live in what is now the USA were Native Americans. They belonged to many different groups, each with its own traditions and beliefs. Beginning in the late 1500s, settlers from European countries began to arrive. From about 1600 to 1750, Europeans settled throughout the eastern part of the present-day USA. Most of them were from the UK, so the new land became a colony of Britain. The population also included large numbers of Dutch people, as well as those from France, Sweden, Germany and most other Western European countries. Some black Africans were brought against their will and put to work as slaves. Descendants of all these people make up the American population today.

Moving westwards

The United States of America was born after the colonists won a war of independence against Britain in 1783. The new country grew steadily over the next 100 years. In 1803, President Thomas Jefferson bought a huge piece of land in the middle of what is now the USA from France, which doubled the size of

◀ *This statue in Jamestown, Virginia, commemorates Captain John Smith, who helped establish the first permanent English settlement in America.*

the country. People began travelling west into lands that had previously been unexplored by Europeans. The US government gave away land on the prairies to people who would farm it. These people became known as homesteaders. The Native Americans, who had once moved freely across these lands, were driven on to controlled areas called reservations.

Waves of immigration

Throughout its history, the USA has welcomed millions of immigrants. From 1820 to 1870, about 7.5 million people arrived, many of them from Ireland and Germany. Then, from 1870 to 1916, about 25 million people moved to the USA, doubling its population. Most of them were from Eastern Europe and from China.

FAMOUS AMERICAN

Jane Addams (1860–1935)

Jane Addams devoted her life to helping immigrants and the poor in the USA. She founded Hull House in Chicago in 1889. Here, immigrants learned the skills they needed to become citizens of the USA. Addams won the Nobel Peace Prize in 1931.

▼ *Immigrants arriving in America in the early twentieth century.*

The population today

In 1960, 83 per cent of Americans were white people who were born there. Most of the rest were black Americans descended from African slaves. By 2006, only 67 per cent of Americans were native-born whites. About 14 per cent were Hispanic (from the Spanish-speaking countries of Central America) and 12 per cent were black. About 12 per cent of the US population were immigrants. This most recent wave of immigration is still going on today.

PLACE IN THE WORLD

Population: **307,212,123**

Percentage of world total: **4.5%**

World ranking: **3rd**

Where do Americans live?

The coastal regions along the Atlantic and Pacific oceans and the Gulf of Mexico are home to about 38 per cent of Americans. About 33 per cent live around the Great Lakes and in the Northeast region. Most of the rest live in the Rocky Mountain and Great Plains states. The area between Boston, Massachusetts and Washington, DC, is the most densely populated.

▼ *Hispanic immigrant workers pick beans in a field in Florida. People like these, from Latin America, make up the latest wave of immigrants to the USA.*

Americans on the move

Americans as a group move around more than people in the rest of the world. The average American moves 11 to 13 times in his or her life, mostly within the USA, but sometimes abroad. As different parts of the USA are made up of people from different ethnic backgrounds, such a mobile population helps Americans become familiar with different cultures, and creates the multicultural society that is typical of the USA.

▲ *The USA is one of the most multicultural countries in the world, with people from many ethnic backgrounds.*

Standard of living

Americans enjoy one of the highest standards of living in the world. But in some ways the USA does not meet the same standards as other developed countries. It has a higher divorce rate, lower educational performance, higher rates of crime and homelessness, and a higher infant mortality rate than many countries in Western Europe, for example.

GLOBAL LEADER

Immigration

The USA leads the world in immigration. In 2007, most newcomers came from Mexico, China, the Philippines, India and El Salvador. Almost a third of the foreign-born people in the USA were from Mexico.

American fast food, pop music, television programmes, movies and clothing styles have spread across the globe. They all influence the culture and lifestyles of millions of people.

Freedom to be different

The people of the USA have a strong sense of shared culture. Most Americans speak English and have similar habits of dress, food and housing. At the same time, Americans descended from the different groups of early settlers are often proud of their individual heritage. The traditions of many countries, brought by millions of immigrants, have blended to create American culture. This makes Americans more tolerant than people in many other countries, and they have a strong belief in equality and freedom.

Personal space

Americans are unique among other Western cultures in their desire to live apart from others. Most Americans prefer to live in suburbs rather than in crowded cities.

▶ *As suburbs grew, shopping malls became popular as a way for people to get everything they needed under one roof.*

IT STARTED HERE

Shopping malls

The first modern, enclosed shopping mall was built in Edina, Minnesota, in 1956. It was the first mall to be built on more than one level and entirely enclosed. It became the model for nearly all shopping malls today.

The American dream

Since the mid 1900s, the typical 'American dream' has been to own a large house in the suburbs with at least one car. After the end of World War II in 1945, there was a large movement of people from the cities to the suburbs. This was largely because there was the space to 'spread out' – the USA is a large country and had not been settled for hundreds of years like many other countries.

A religious nation

People are free to follow any religion they want. Surveys show that about seven in 10 Americans believe in God, and around half of them say that religion is very important in their lives. More than 80 per cent of Americans call themselves Christians, although not all of them are practising.

IT'S A FACT!

Christian churches in America have grown bigger over the last 20 years. A megachurch is a Christian church with more than 2,000 members. Services usually feature live music and videos projected on large screens. In 2008, there were about 1,360 megachurches in the USA. About five million people attend services at megachurches across America each week.

▼ *This megachurch in Illinois can seat 7,000 people. Big screens allow everyone to see the preacher and to share in the experience.*

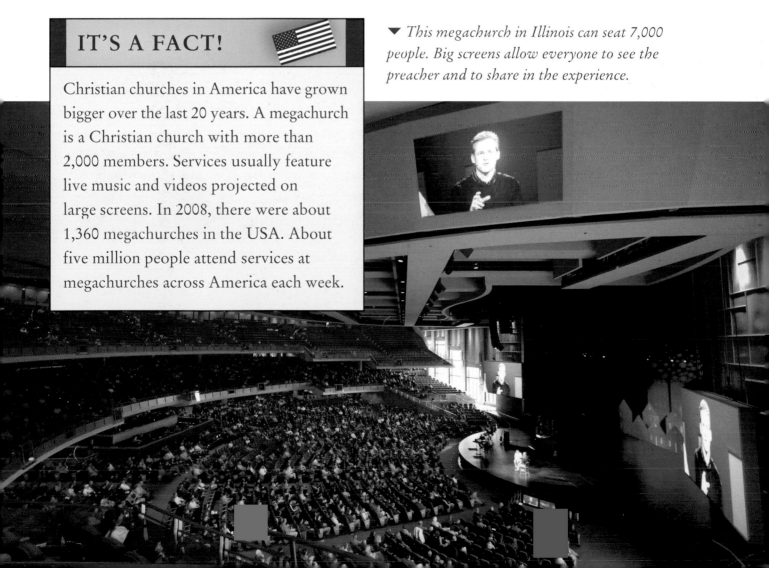

Festivals and celebrations

One of the most important national holidays in the USA is Independence Day, celebrated on 4 July every year to commemorate the adoption of the Declaration of Independence and freedom from British rule. Families and friends have picnics, and there are often fireworks displays. Thanksgiving is a harvest festival celebrated in November, to commemorate the Native Americans helping the early settlers by sharing their food with them.

GOING GLOBAL

Fast food, which started in America, has exploded around the world. McDonald's has 30,000 restaurants worldwide in 119 countries. KFC, the fried chicken chain, is especially popular in China, where it operates 800 stores.

A sporting nation

Americans are huge sports fans and sport is an important part of American culture. The most popular sports are American football, baseball, basketball and ice hockey, and the USA leads the world in these sports. Americans support their teams passionately, and championship games such as the Super Bowl (American football) and the World Series (baseball) attract thousands of fans to the live event and millions more who watch on television. Soccer – the most popular sport in the world – is not nearly as popular as other sports in the USA.

▼ *Crowds in the National Mall park in Washington, D.C. celebrate Independence Day on 4 July. Families gather for picnics and to watch fireworks after the sun sets.*

Film and music

American popular culture such as films, television and musical styles are its most famous exports. As the home of Hollywood, America has influenced the film industry in many other countries, but it is also known for creating high-quality television dramas that are popular all over the world. Musical genres such as jazz, blues and country music were all born in the USA. Later, these were adapted and developed into modern styles such as rock 'n' roll, rap, soul and funk. Today, American film and pop stars are known all over the world, and are more famous than native stars in many countries.

THE HOME OF...

Hollywood

The area of Los Angeles, California, known as Hollywood is the heart of the world's film industry. The first film studio was set up here in 1909, and since then Hollywood has set the standard for blockbuster movies all over the world, making and releasing hundreds of films every year. Its influence is so widespread that the Indian film industry based in Mumbai has been nicknamed 'Bollywood'.

The USA has by far the largest economy in the world. The country is rich in resources, including fertile farmland, waterways, minerals and forests. In 2008, it produced about US$15 billion worth of goods and services. But hard times struck and the USA suffered a recession, which spread around the world.

Free enterprise

The economy of the USA is based on free enterprise. This means that the people rather than the government manage the economy. The government makes some rules and laws, and controls some business activities to make sure that businesses operate fairly and that Americans get the goods and services they need for a safe, happy life. However, the people decide what to make, and how to make it; they decide what to sell, and for how much money.

▼ *Bill Gates – one of the richest men in the world – shows off Microsoft's Tablet PC.*

FAMOUS AMERICAN

Bill Gates (b. 1955)

Bill Gates is a pioneer in the personal-computer industry. With a boyhood friend, Paul Allen, he founded Microsoft in 1975. They developed operating systems – programs that tell computers how to run. Today, Microsoft is the world's largest software company, selling the world's top operating system, Windows.

Growing service industries

As in other Western countries, the American service industry employs most of the workers and creates most of the country's wealth. Service industries are those that provide services for people rather than making products. In the early 2000s, 83 per cent of America's workers were employed in service industries, including property, tourism, healthcare, hotels, law firms, banking and restaurants.

PLACE IN THE WORLD

Value of economy:
US$14.29 trillion

Percentage of world total: **21%**

World ranking: **1st**

Hi-tech leader

The USA has long been known as a leader in technology, and this brings a lot of money into the economy. For the most part, it has led the world in advances in computers, medicine, spacecraft, air travel and military equipment. In particular, it led the way in space technology. America was the first country to put a man on the Moon, and it now plays an important part in the International Space Station (ISS), a joint project between the USA, Russia, Japan, Canada and countries of the European Space Agency.

▼ *An American astronaut and one from the European Space Agency work on the ISS, an international space project.*

Global economy

The USA is both the world's biggest importer and the world's biggest exporter of goods and services. Recently, the US economy has become more tied up with that of other countries. For example, US companies import parts such as car parts from other countries. The vehicles are put together in the USA and the finished products are shipped abroad to be sold. The USA's top trading partners in 2008 were Canada, China, Mexico, Japan and Germany.

▲ *The Port of Miami is one of the largest in the USA. Both container ships for importing and exporting goods, and cruise ships use this port.*

Manufacturing

Businesses that produce goods such as steel, cars, computers, toys and clothing are called manufacturers. The USA is the world leader in manufacturing, and American products – from Apple iPods and Disney merchandise to clothing – can be found everywhere. However, there are now fewer workers in the manufacturing industry than ever before. Over the past 30 years, many American companies have built factories in other countries, such as China, Mexico and India, where labour costs are lower. This means that many American manufacturing jobs have been lost.

GOING GLOBAL

American children play with mostly foreign-made toys. Almost 90 per cent of all toys sold in the USA are imported, and China supplies more than three-quarters of the toys sold there.

The tourist industry

Tourism is big business in the USA. In fact, America earns more from tourists than any other country in the world. In 2007, tourism brought nearly US$98 billion into the US economy. Because the USA is such a large country, it has many different attractions for tourists. Some come to enjoy the sunshine and beaches in places like California, or to go to world-famous amusement parks like Disneyland. Others visit the many national parks and natural sites like the Grand Canyon. Still others visit big cities like New York to go to the museums and galleries – or just to enjoy the shopping.

Economic hard times

In 2007, the US economy seemed strong, but there were signs of trouble. Prices for items like petrol and services such as healthcare were rising, but people's wages were not rising. By late 2008, many businesses, including major banks and car companies, had failed. People started to compare this economic crisis to the Great Depression – a period of severe economic hardship that lasted from the late 1920s to the late 1930s. In 2008 and early 2009, the US government spent more than US$1.2 trillion to rescue troubled companies and create projects to put people to work.

▼ *Disneyland, California, is one of the world's top tourist attractions, with around 15 million visitors per year.*

Government and politics

The USA was formed a little more than 230 years ago, but its constitution – the document that describes the basic principles of how the country will be run – is the oldest written constitution still in use. It has lasted such a long time because it has ensured a stable government and a good life for most Americans.

Power from the people

According to the constitution, the power is held by the people of America. It states clearly what powers the government has, which include the authority to collect taxes, to maintain the armed forces and to carry on trade with other countries. The constitution also limits the power of the government by granting American citizens certain rights. For example, the government cannot tell people what religion they must follow or punish people for what they say or write publicly.

THE HOME OF...

The White House

The White House is the home and official workplace of the US president. It is situated in Washington, DC, and was built between 1792 and 1800. Not far from the White House is the United States Capitol, which is where Congress – the Senate and the House of Representatives – meets.

▼ *The White House has become a global symbol of democracy.*

Federal system

The USA has a federal system of government. This means that the country is made up of separate states united under the federal, or national, government. Each state can make its own laws on matters such as education or punishments for crimes, but state laws cannot conflict with laws passed by the federal government – and all laws must follow the rules of the constitution.

Three branches of government

The US government is made up of three branches: executive, legislative and judicial. The president of the USA is the leader of the executive branch, which carries out the laws. Two groups of lawmakers – the House of Representatives and the Senate – make up the legislative branch. They write and pass new laws. The judicial branch is made up of courts led by judges. The judicial branch settles disagreements about laws. It also decides whether laws passed by the House and Senate follow the rules of the US constitution. Each branch of the government can undo actions by the other branches, which makes sure that no one branch can grow too powerful.

▲ *The United States Congress is jointly made up of the House of Representatives and the Senate. The men and women of Congress are elected by the people in their home state.*

World superpower

The USA's position as the world's only superpower means that it has a lot of influence over international affairs. Other countries will often follow the USA's lead in matters of war, international politics and economic policy, and decisions made in the USA can have a far-reaching effect. The power the USA has makes it a model for other nations, but it also sometimes makes it a target for criticism.

Terrorist attacks

On 11 September 2001, Islamic terrorists destroyed the World Trade Center, two large office towers in New York City. In response to this, the US government declared a 'War on Terror', determined to catch the people who had carried out the attacks and prevent such an event happening again.

GOING GLOBAL

The US government suspected that Iraq was involved in the terrorist attacks and claimed that the country had weapons of mass destruction. The USA invaded Iraq in 2003 and overthrew its leader, Saddam Hussein. Several other countries were drawn into the war. The UK, Australia, Poland and Denmark also sent troops to Iraq, but countries such as France, Germany and Russia were against the invasion.

▲ *Firefighters search through the rubble after the 9/11 terrorist attacks in New York.*

The War on Terror

To prevent another terrorist attack on US soil, the government took drastic measures. It passed laws making it legal to spy on Americans. It started wars in Iraq and Afghanistan, where Islamic terrorists were believed to be. It also imprisoned many suspected terrorists in a prison camp at Guantanamo Bay in Cuba.

Promising change

When Barack Obama became president in January 2009, he promised to change many policies that Americans were unhappy with. In particular he announced that he would bring all troops home from Iraq by 2010. He ordered the release of records proving that the United States government had previously carried out widespread torture of prisoners. President Obama also promised to close the prison at Guantanamo Bay. He made a visit to the Middle East in June 2009 in an effort to improve relations with the Islamic world.

FAMOUS AMERICAN

Barack Obama (b. 1961)

Barack Obama grew up in Hawaii and Indonesia, the son of an American mother and a Kenyan father. He entered politics in 1996 when he was elected to the Illinois Senate, and in 2005 he became a US senator. In January 2009, he became the US president – the first African-American to hold that position.

▶ *Many Americans felt that President Barack Obama's election was a turning point for the country, and that the political and economic situation would begin to improve.*

It is likely that the USA will continue to be the world's most powerful nation for some years, despite the rise of China as a global power. Over the next few years, Americans' living standards may improve, but those in other countries may become more equal to the USA. The US population will also change, as immigration rises and the birth rate slows.

Changing face of the nation

In 2005, about 12 per cent of the US population was foreign-born. By 2050, that number is expected to rise to 19 per cent. It is estimated that 67 million people will immigrate to the USA in the next 40 years. By 2020, it is thought that the number of children of foreign-born Hispanics will have doubled from what it was in 2000. These people may not have equal education and job opportunities with other groups, so the gap between rich and poor may grow wider.

▼ *Immigrant children hold up the certificates that prove they are now American citizens.*

Population growth

Unlike many developed countries in Europe and Asia, where populations are declining, the population of the USA is still growing. People are also living longer than ever before, and in coming years, the number of senior citizens will grow. By 2020 the US Census Bureau expects that about one in every five people will be 65 or older. There will be fewer younger workers to create wealth for the country, so the USA will be challenged to find ways to care for its ageing population. More older Americans will also be working well beyond today's retirement age of 65.

The future of trade

Most experts believe that all over the world, trade among different countries will go up. The USA will continue to be a part of that growth. In 2007, imports made up about 17 per cent of the total US economy. Exports of American-made products were about 12 per cent. The US government believes that by 2027, this will have grown dramatically, and imports will be about 26 per cent of the US economy and exports will be about 27 per cent.

▲ *Schoolchildren say the Pledge of Allegiance before the US flag. Young people (under the age of 20) currently make up a quarter of the US population, but that balance is expected to shift in the near future.*

Glossary

Christianity a religion that follows the teachings of Jesus Christ.

colony a territory under the immediate political control of a nation.

conservation protecting and preserving the natural environment and wildlife.

constitution a document that lays out the main laws of a nation. Laws are not allowed to be passed that contradict a country's constitution.

continent one of the Earth's seven great land masses – Africa, Antarctica, Asia, Australia, Europe, North America and South America.

democracy a form of government in which people vote for the leaders they wish to represent them.

economy the financial system of a country or region, including how much money is made from the production and sale of goods and services.

ethnic group a group of people who identify with each other and feel they share a history.

export to transport products or materials abroad for sale or trade.

immigrant a person who has moved to another country to live.

import to bring in goods or materials from a foreign country for sale.

infant mortality the number of children who die before reaching adulthood in a particular country.

minerals natural rocks that come from the ground.

plateau a relatively flat, high expanse of land.

pollution spoiling the environment with man-made waste, such as gases from vehicle emissions or chemicals from factories or pesticides.

prairie a large expanse of grassland, where few trees grow.

rainforest a forest that receives more than 1 m (3.3 ft) of rainfall spread evenly throughout the year.

recession an extended period when the economy of a country slows down.

reservations special areas of land set aside for the Native American people after they were driven off their native land by white settlers.

resources things that are available to use, often to help develop a country's industry and economy. Resources could be minerals, workers (labour), water, or many other things.

suburbs areas on the outskirts of cities that are less built-up than city centres.

terrorist a person who uses violence or causes fear, to try and change a political system or policy.

USSR Union of Soviet Socialist Republics. A communist country in eastern Europe and northern Asia. In 1991, the USSR split into independent countries, including Russia.

Further information

Books

Attack on America (Dates with History)
by Brian Williams
(Cherrytree Books, 2007)

Celebrate USA
by Robyn Hardyman
(Franklin Watts, 2009)

The USA (Looking at Countries)
by Kathleen Pohl
(Franklin Watts, 2009)

USA (Letters from Around the World)
by Cath Senker
(Cherrytree Books, 2007)

Websites

http://www.americaslibrary.gov/cgi-bin/page.cgi
The Library of Congress site with information for kids about American people, states and historical events.

http://www.travelforkids.com/Funtodo/United_States/usa.htm
Take a journey through the USA with this fun site, travelling from Alaska to Hawaii.

http://www.socialstudiesforkids.com/subjects/economics.htm
Get to grips with economics with this site, where topics such as money, trade and budgets are explained.

Every effort has been made by the publisher to ensure that these websites contain no inappropriate or offensive material. However, because of the nature of the Internet, it is impossible to guarantee that the content of these sites will not be altered. We strongly advise that Internet access is supervised by a responsible adult.

Index

Numbers in **bold** indicate pictures

ATLAS OF WORLD ISSUES

ATLAS OF WORLD ISSUES

DR NICK MIDDLETON

Lecturer in Physical Geography
Oriel College & St. Anne's College
Oxford University

Oxford University Press 1988

Published by

Oxford University Press, Walton Street, Oxford OX2 6DP
Oxford New York Toronto Delhi Bombay Calcutta Madras
Karachi Petaling Jaya Singapore Hong Kong Tokyo Nairobi
Dar es Salaam Cape Town Melbourne Auckland

and associated companies in Berlin and Ibadan
Oxford is a trademark of Oxford University Press

First Published in U.K. in 1988
Reprinted 1990, 1991

Illustrated by Mike Saunders/Thorogood Burgess,
Engineering Surveys Reproduction Limited, UK,
Janos Marffy/Thorogood Burgess,
Peter Sarson and Tony Bryant

Cover artwork by Steve Weston

ISBN 0 19 913335 2

Typesetting by Opus, Oxford
Colour separations by Columbia Offset
Printed in Spain by Salingraf S.A.L.

Created and produced by Ilex Publishers Limited
29–31 George Street, Oxford OX1 2AJ

Contents

1 Physical World

The earth is covered by water (70%) and land (30%). This land and sea is sitting on the earth's crust, which is divided into a number of plates floating on the molten rock below known as the 'mantle'.

These plates move, and the margins between the plates are areas of 'seismic' activity: volcanoes and earthquakes (see Indonesia and Japan below). Where plates move apart or 'diverge' beneath the oceans, upwelling molten rock forms a ridge. Where plates collide or 'converge' beneath the oceans, a trench is formed as one plate slides beneath another. At places where convergence occurs on land the edge of a plate becomes crumbled, building a chain of mountains such as where the Indian Plate is colliding with the Eurasian Plate. This is creating the Himalayas, the world's highest mountain range (see below).

Drifting continents
About 200 million years ago the continents we know from today's world map were all joined as a sort of supercontinent, called 'Pangaea' (top). This original landmass split in two and began to move. As time continued other continents broke away and India began moving towards Asia (middle). Today India has collided with Asia, and is still moving northward. The edges of the Indian and Eurasian plates have crumpled to form the Himalayas (below).

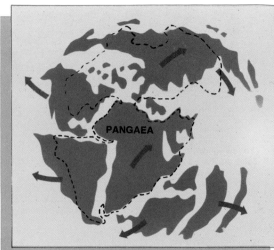

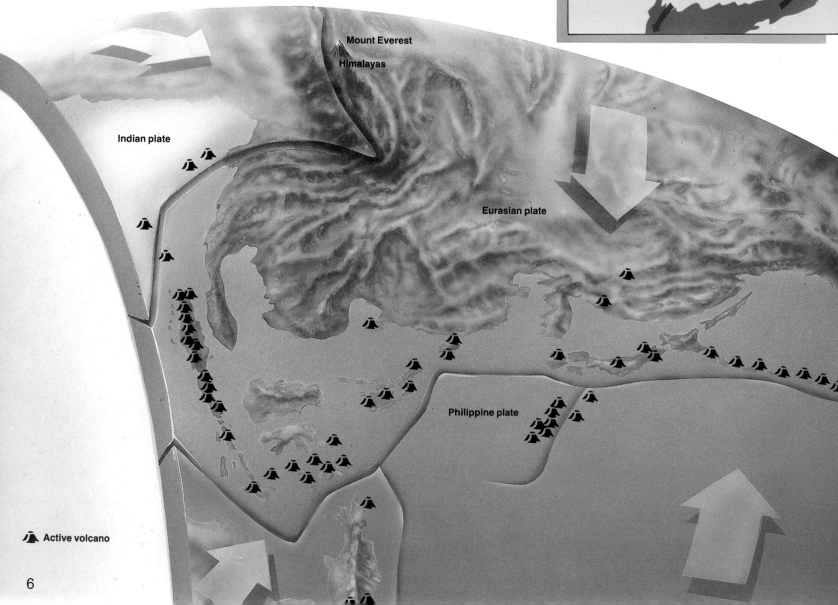

Mount Everest

Himalayas

Indian plate

Eurasian plate

Philippine plate

🌋 **Active volcano**

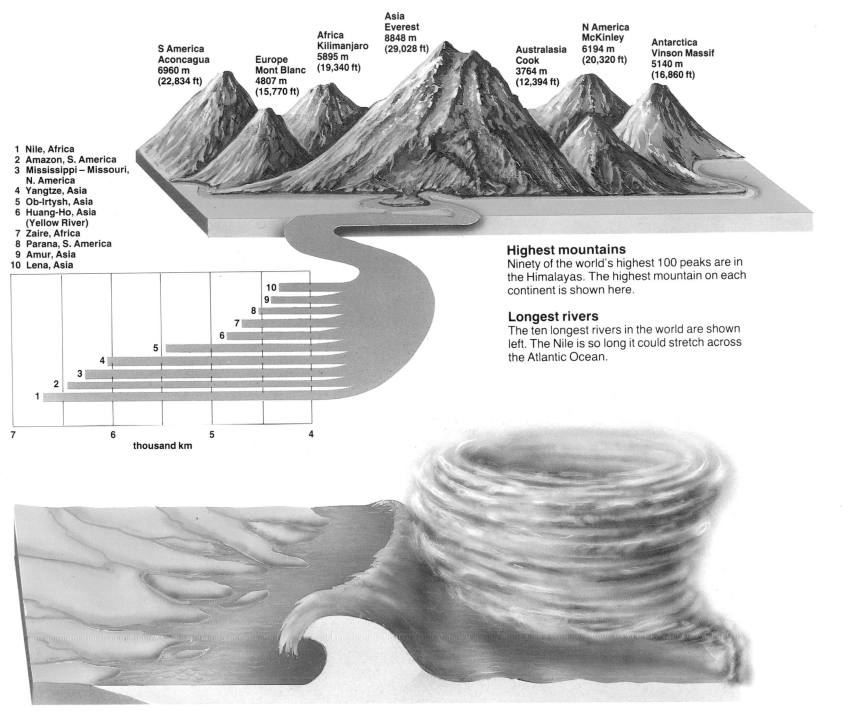

Highest mountains
Ninety of the world's highest 100 peaks are in the Himalayas. The highest mountain on each continent is shown here.

S America
Aconcagua
6960 m
(22,834 ft)

Europe
Mont Blanc
4807 m
(15,770 ft)

Africa
Kilimanjaro
5895 m
(19,340 ft)

Asia
Everest
8848 m
(29,028 ft)

Australasia
Cook
3764 m
(12,394 ft)

N America
McKinley
6194 m
(20,320 ft)

Antarctica
Vinson Massif
5140 m
(16,860 ft)

1 Nile, Africa
2 Amazon, S. America
3 Mississippi – Missouri, N. America
4 Yangtze, Asia
5 Ob-Irtysh, Asia
6 Huang-Ho, Asia (Yellow River)
7 Zaire, Africa
8 Parana, S. America
9 Amur, Asia
10 Lena, Asia

thousand km

Longest rivers
The ten longest rivers in the world are shown left. The Nile is so long it could stretch across the Atlantic Ocean.

Natural Hazards: Bangladesh
In Bangladesh 80 per cent of the land is a floodplain. The country is one of the most densely populated in Asia (see POPULATION) and millions of people live on this low-lying land where flooding occurs almost every year. The flooding problems of Bangladesh have been made worse by deforestation in the Himalayas. In the last decade or so tree cutting on slopes in India and Nepal has resulted in widespread soil erosion. This soil is brought to Bangladesh by the River Ganges and is deposited at the delta, making new islands. This new land is quickly colonised by land-hungry people, but the islands are in the most hazardous areas and are very prone to flooding. This flooding occurs either during the monsoon rains (July – Sept) or from tropical storms (Nov – May).

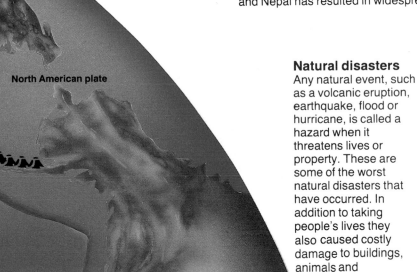

North American plate

Natural disasters
Any natural event, such as a volcanic eruption, earthquake, flood or hurricane, is called a hazard when it threatens lives or property. These are some of the worst natural disasters that have occurred. In addition to taking people's lives they also caused costly damage to buildings, animals and agricultural land.

Disaster	Location and date	Deaths
Circular Storm	Ganges Delta Islands, Bangladesh. November 1970	1,000,000
Flood	Huang-Ho, China October 1887	900,000
Earthquake	Shensi Province, China. January 1556	830,000
Landslide	Kansu Province, China December 1920	180,000
Volcanic Eruption	Tambora Sumbawa, Indonesia. April 1815	92,000
Avalanche	Yungay, Huascarán, Peru May 1970	18,000

2 Climate

Climate can be thought of as the yearly average of the day-to-day weather experienced at a particular place. The earth's climates are caused by movements and regular changes in the lowest level of the atmosphere, known as the 'troposphere'.

In general terms, the earth's atmosphere can be thought of as a giant heat engine that is continually working to smooth out the differences in the heat energy received from the sun at different places on earth. The equator is closer to the sun than the poles and is, therefore, hotter. If this imbalance remained then the equator would get gradually hotter and hotter, and the poles would get colder and colder. Movements of the air, and the oceans, act to redistribute this heat imbalance.

In practice variations in altitude, position of land and sea and the time of year all affect climate, as well as the sun's warmth. These other factors all affect temperature, rainfall, winds, humidity, evaporation and other elements that make up a particular area's climate.

Average temperatures and wind patterns in January and July
The wind patterns are the dominant ones that blow at the earth's surface. At different heights above the ground the winds often blow in different directions and at different speeds (see right).

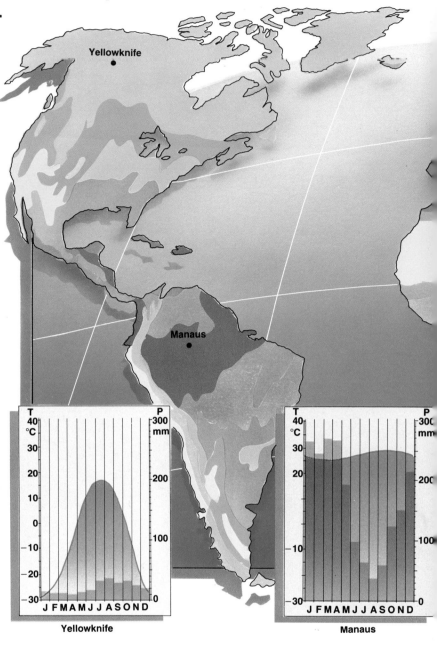

Yellowknife

Manaus

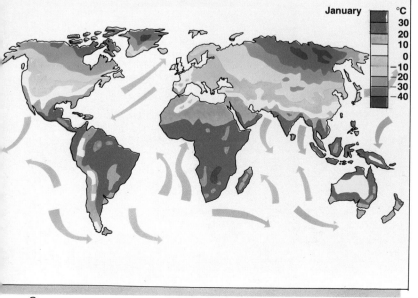

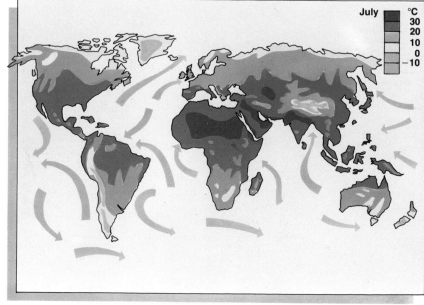

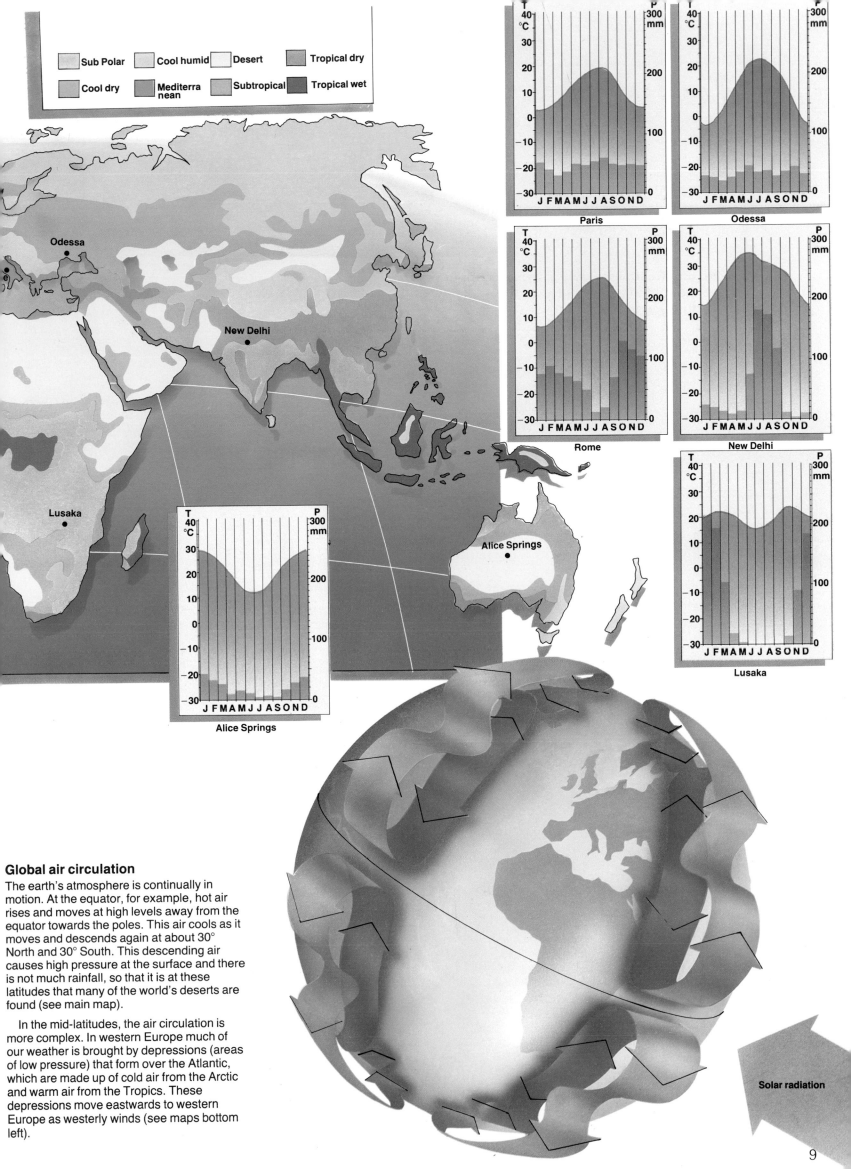

Legend:
- Sub Polar
- Cool dry
- Cool humid
- Mediterranean
- Desert
- Subtropical
- Tropical dry
- Tropical wet

Paris

Odessa

Rome

New Delhi

Alice Springs

Lusaka

Global air circulation

The earth's atmosphere is continually in motion. At the equator, for example, hot air rises and moves at high levels away from the equator towards the poles. This air cools as it moves and descends again at about 30° North and 30° South. This descending air causes high pressure at the surface and there is not much rainfall, so that it is at these latitudes that many of the world's deserts are found (see main map).

In the mid-latitudes, the air circulation is more complex. In western Europe much of our weather is brought by depressions (areas of low pressure) that form over the Atlantic, which are made up of cold air from the Arctic and warm air from the Tropics. These depressions move eastwards to western Europe as westerly winds (see maps bottom left).

Solar radiation

9

3 Vegetation

Almost the entire earth's land surface supports some kind of plant life, the exception being those areas permanently covered by ice. Today, about 1.7 million plant species have been identified and recorded, just a small proportion of the estimated total number of species, which is between five and ten million.

The type and cover of vegetation varies greatly across the world and depends to a large extent on the climate of an area and the type of soil. For example, the cold tundra regions of northern Canada and the northern Soviet Union are typically grasslands with mosses and lichens. The ground is often frozen or marshy. Hot deserts, by contrast, have many bare areas of ground with cacti, thorny bushes and wiry grass. A tropical rain forest has very dense vegetation with many layers: high trees, shrubs and ground plants.

Human land use has modified vegetation patterns for thousands of years. Agriculture involves clearing natural vegetation and sowing new plants, and as settlements grow land is cleared for new dwellings. As the world population grows and the methods for vegetation clearance and modification become more efficient, so our ability to modify or destroy vegetation increases. The world's tropical rain forests are being cleared at a rate of 80,000 square kilometres each year, an area the size of Austria. Such rapid and large scale destruction of vegetation has serious consequences (see below right).

Solar Energy

Photosynthesis

Food

Fuelwood

Building Material

Shelter

Soil stabilised

Conversion of Minerals

Vegetation's role

Vegetation uses the sun's energy and nutrients from the soil to grow. It also protects the soil from erosion and provides food and shelter for animals. Many plants provide us with the food we eat, of course, but vegetation is also used for fuel, building material and many other products.

Vegetation zones

This map shows the world's natural vegetation zones, but in many areas human populations have changed the natural vegetation. Perhaps most important in this respect is the effect of agriculture: compare this map with the map of agricultural zones in FOOD AND WATER.

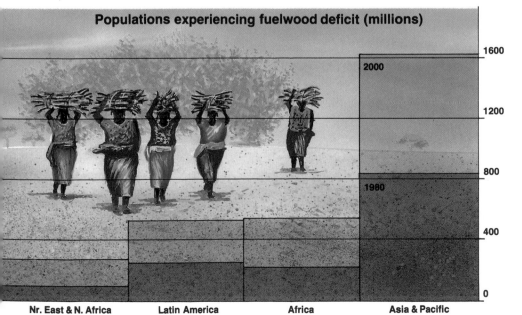

Populations experiencing fuelwood deficit (millions)

2000

1980

1600
1200
800
400
0

Nr. East & N. Africa   Latin America   Africa   Asia & Pacific

Fuelwood scarcity

Many people in the developing countries collect wood from around their settlements to use for cooking and heating. They gather dead wood from the ground or cut off twigs and branches. In some areas demand is so great that whole trees are felled. These trees are rarely replanted, so that reserves are depleted and the soil is open to increased erosion. Estimates suggest that 1.3 billion people in the Third World are short of fuelwood. By the year 2000 this figure is expected to reach three billion.

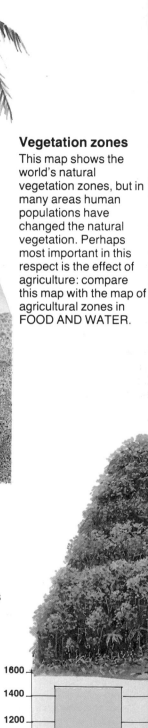

1600
1400
1200
1000
800
600
400
200
0

Brazil

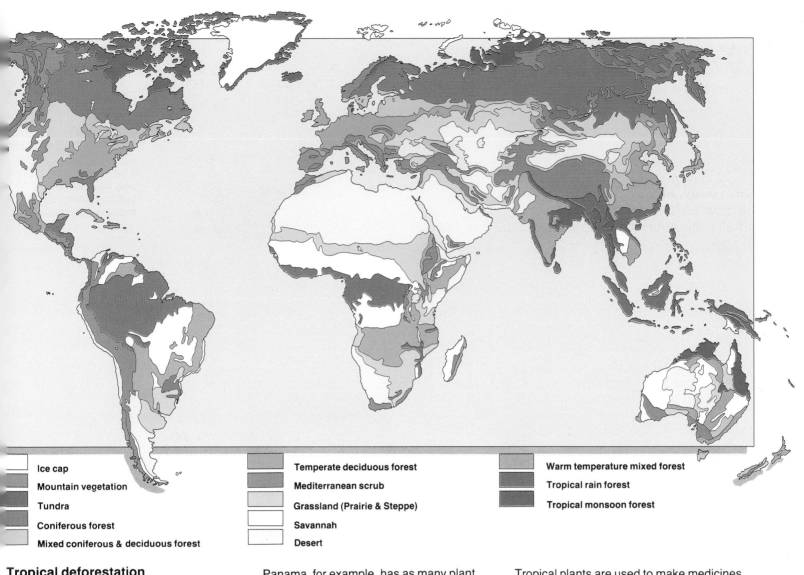

Ice cap	Temperate deciduous forest	Warm temperature mixed forest
Mountain vegetation	Mediterranean scrub	Tropical rain forest
Tundra	Grassland (Prairie & Steppe)	Tropical monsoon forest
Coniferous forest	Savannah	
Mixed coniferous & deciduous forest	Desert	

Tropical deforestation

Tropical rain forests cover 7% of the earth's land area, yet they are home to half of all its species. They hold a tremendous diversity of species: the Central American state of Panama, for example, has as many plant species as the whole of Europe.

Destruction of these forests means the loss of untold numbers of potential new resources.

Tropical plants are used to make medicines and industrial products. These forests are also home to 200 million people, who stand to lose their homelands. Massive soil erosion often follows tree clearance.

Rates of clearance

Area deforested each year (thousand hectares)

Indonesia   Colombia   India   Thailand   Ivory Coast   Costa Rica

4 Nations

These are the independent nations of the world today. Many of the countries on this map, particularly in Africa, are fairly new, having gained independence from the colonial empires of European countries. The central African state of Zaire, for example, was the Belgian Congo until 1960 when it became independent. In 1971 its name was changed to Zaire.

In addition to these countries there are 59 other territories that are governed in part by other nations. Greenland, for example, is part of the European country of Denmark. Hong Kong is currently an overseas territory of the United Kingdom, although it will become part of China again on July 1, 1997.

The large majority of these countries are members of the United Nations (UN), 159 states in all. The UN is the largest of a number of alliances for international co-operation. There are many others formed for political, cultural, economic and defence purposes. Some of the main ones are also shown here.

European Community

Also known as the European Economic Community (EEC) or the Common Market, the European Community was set up in 1957 with six members. The Community makes economic and political agreements between its members to serve their common interests. Today the Community has 12 member nations.

NATO   Warsaw Pact

NATO

The North Atlantic Treaty Organisation (NATO) is an alliance that deals with the defence of its Western country members.

Warsaw Pact

The Warsaw Pact, first signed in 1955, is a treaty for help and co-operation in military matters. It has seven members, the six most closely allied East European Communist countries with the USSR as its head.

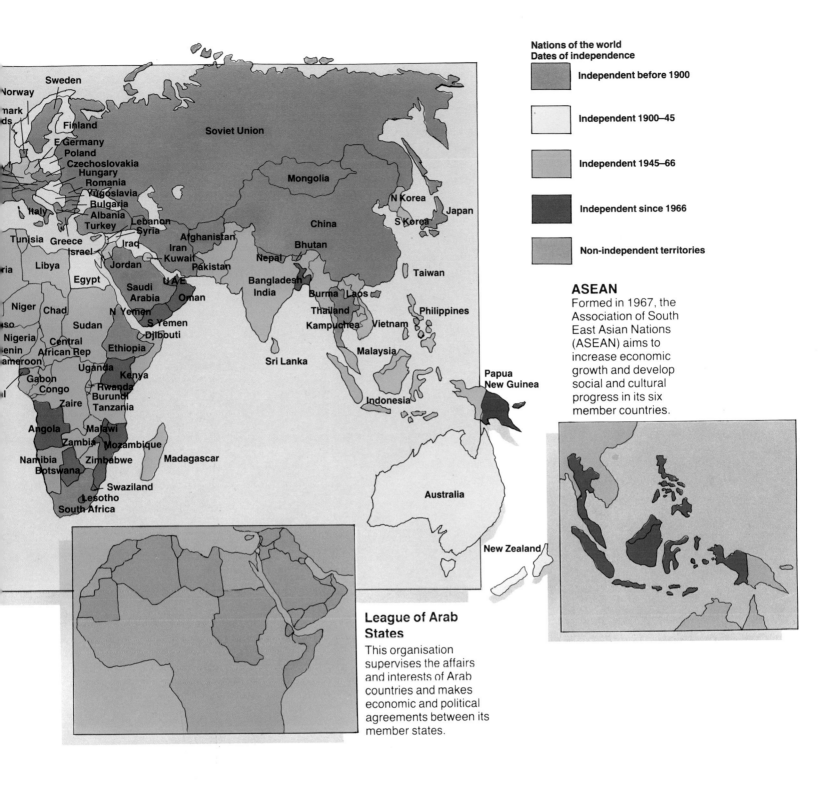

**Nations of the world
Dates of independence**

Independent before 1900

Independent 1900–45

Independent 1945–66

Independent since 1966

Non-independent territories

Sweden
Norway
mark
ds
Finland
E Germany
Poland
Czechoslovakia
Hungary
Romania
Yugoslavia
Italy
Bulgaria
Albania
Turkey
Lebanon
Syria
Tunisia
Greece
Israel
Iraq
Libya
Jordan
Egypt
Saudi Arabia
Niger
Chad
N Yemen
Sudan
S Yemen
Nigeria
Central African Rep
enin
Djibouti
ameroon
Ethiopia
Gabon
Uganda
Congo
Kenya
Rwanda
Burundi
Zaire
Tanzania
Angola
Malawi
Zambia
Mozambique
Namibia
Zimbabwe
Madagascar
Botswana
Swaziland
Lesotho
South Africa

Soviet Union
Mongolia
N Korea
S Korea
Japan
China
Afghanistan
Iran
Bhutan
Kuwait
Pakistan
Nepal
UAE
Oman
Bangladesh
India
Taiwan
Burma
Laos
Thailand
Philippines
Kampuchea
Vietnam
Sri Lanka
Malaysia
Papua New Guinea
Indonesia
Australia
New Zealand

ASEAN

Formed in 1967, the Association of South East Asian Nations (ASEAN) aims to increase economic growth and develop social and cultural progress in its six member countries.

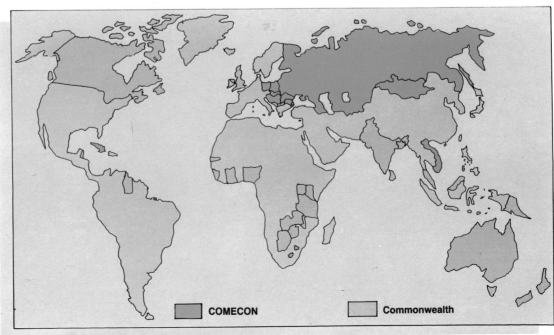

League of Arab States

This organisation supervises the affairs and interests of Arab countries and makes economic and political agreements between its member states.

The Commonwealth

The 49 member states of the Commonwealth are united with Queen Elizabeth II as the Head. These countries were all once part of the British Empire but are now independent nations who co-operate in matters of international affairs, culture and economics.

COMECON

Established in 1949, this organisation of socialist countries aims to help the development of the national economies of its member states.

COMECON   Commonwealth

13

5 Pollution

Pollution is the introduction of harmful substances into the environment by human populations.

It takes many different forms, affecting the land, the sea and the air. For example, tips of household rubbish – tin cans, plastic and so on – pollute the environment, as do factories and motor cars that pump gases and small particles into the atmosphere. Factories also release harmful liquids into rivers that flow into the sea, while spills of oil from ocean-going tankers further pollute the marine environment.

The environment may be polluted in less direct ways. Loud noise, from industries or aeroplanes passing overhead is pollution. Similarly, the temperature of water and other liquids that factories and power stations pump into rivers can be harmful to fish and other forms of aquatic life.

The effects of pollution may be directly harmful to human health. For instance lead from car exhaust fumes can cause brain damage in children. Alternatively, pollution causes damage to plants and animals that form important links in the complicated chain of relationships that makes up the world's environment.

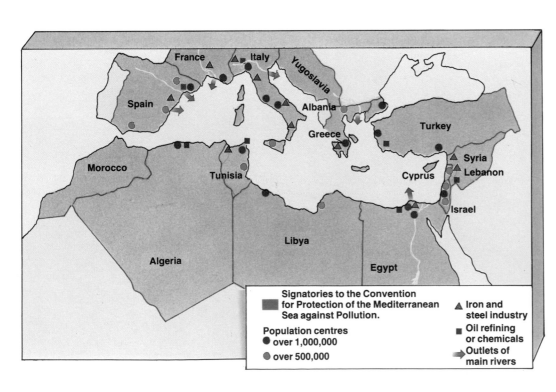

The dirty Mediterranean

The Mediterranean Sea is almost totally enclosed, has very low tides and takes over 70 years to renew its waters completely. It is, therefore, very vulnerable to pollutants, as they tend to accumulate.

Over 100 million people live on the Mediterranean coast and islands, and each year an incredible 430 billion tonnes of pollution reaches their sea from industries, homes and ships.

Signatories to the Convention for Protection of the Mediterranean Sea against Pollution.

Population centres
● over 1,000,000
● over 500,000

▲ Iron and steel industry

■ Oil refining or chemicals

➔ Outlets of main rivers

3

Acid rain

Acid rain is a major environmental pollution problem in the heavily industrialised areas of Europe and North America. It also effects areas outside the industrial centres as the wind carries pollutants over great distances.

1. Burning of fossil fuels produces sulphur and nitrogen oxides, as well as ash, smoke and dust.
2. Dry deposition of acids speeds up the weathering of building stones and chemically attacks plants.
3. Wet deposition (acid rain or snow) may also attack plants and other living things. Acid rain falls on plants, and the ground surface, thus entering the soil, rivers and lakes.
4. The main areas at risk from acid rain in Europe and North America.

The greenhouse effect

1. Carbon dioxide (CO_2) is a natural part of the air we breathe. In normal circumstances energy from the sun is absorbed by the earth as heat. Most of this heat is radiated away from the earth, some warms up the atmosphere, some escapes back into space.

2. For the last 100 years or so the increasing use of fossil fuels has put more CO_2 into the atmosphere. This has raised world temperatures by about $\frac{1}{2}°C$ as CO_2 in the air absorbs more of the heat radiated from the earth, so warming up the atmosphere. There are fears that as CO_2 continues to build up in the earth's atmosphere, world temperatures will continue to rise. This could have disastrous results: ice caps at the poles could melt and flood many parts of the world's coast that are presently above sea level.

6 The Increasing Desert

We use the word 'desertification' to mean 'the making of a desert'. The process occurs on the boundaries of today's deserts. Desertification means that the land produces less food, sustains fewer livestock – and feeds fewer people.

In many cases human beings themselves are responsible for desertification. Some of the most common ways in which local populations misuse their land are by overgrazing, overcultivation and the clearing of vegetation for agricultural purposes and for fuel wood. This mismanagement is often caused by increasing populations and natural factors, such as the occurrence of seasonal dryness or drought.

Desertification usually happens first in the savannah grasslands beyond the desert's edge – but these small areas enlarge and link up, to give the impression of an advancing desert 'wall'.

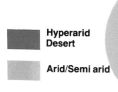

■ **Hyperarid Desert**

░ **Arid/Semi arid**

The Sahel

This is the semi-arid region on the southern fringe of the Sahara Desert in North Africa. It stretches from Mauritania in the west to Sudan and Ethiopia in the east. The area experienced a severe drought from the late-1960s to the mid-1980s.

The map right shows desert encroachment in northern Sudan.

▬ Desert boundary 1958

╌╌ Desert Boundary 1975

◢ Protruding area with many mobile dunes in 1975

╌╌ Border

⤚ Wadi, dry stream bed

● Town

▲ Mountain

World desertification

The map shows the areas of the world that are at risk from desertification. They are mainly around the edge of deserts.

Wadi Haifa

20°N

Dongola● R. Nile

Atbara●

16°N   1959

1975   ● Khartoum

● El Fasher   El Obeid ●

Kosti ●

▲ JMarra

16

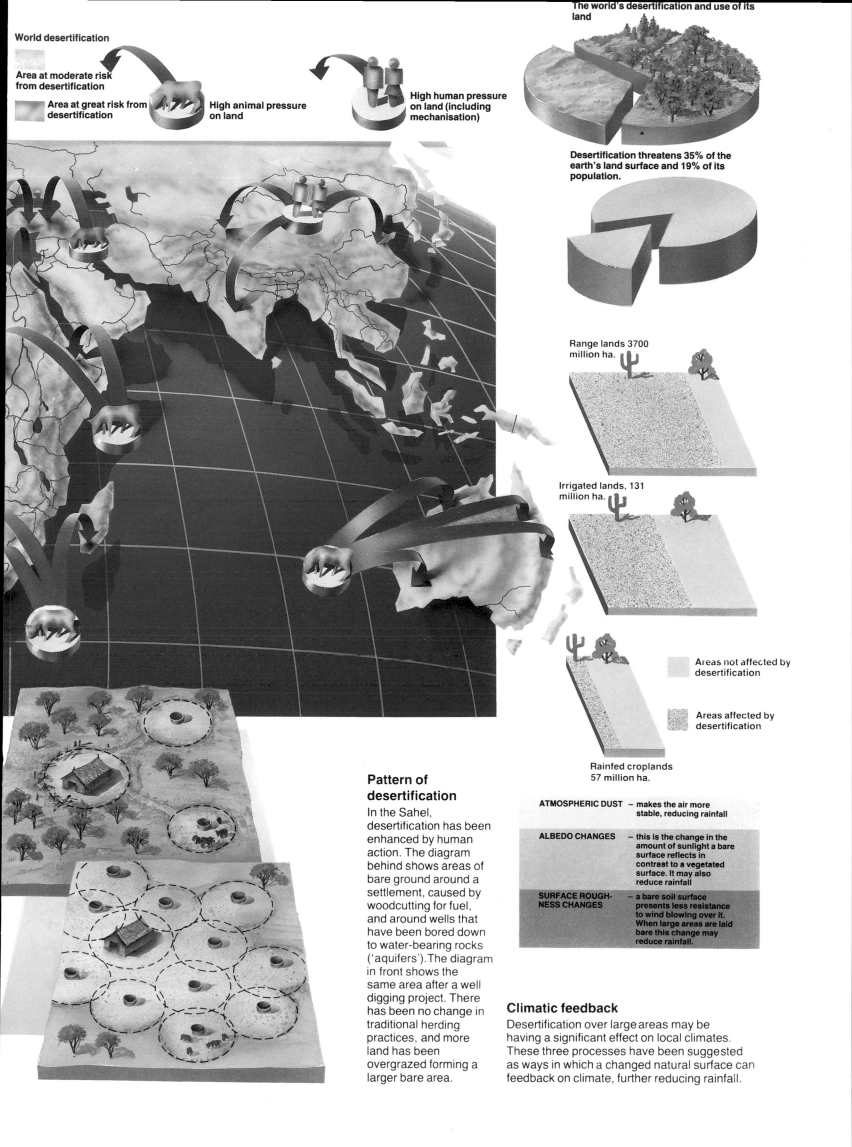

World desertification

Area at moderate risk from desertification

Area at great risk from desertification

High animal pressure on land

High human pressure on land (including mechanisation)

The world's desertification and use of its land

Desertification threatens 35% of the earth's land surface and 19% of its population.

Range lands 3700 million ha.

Irrigated lands, 131 million ha.

Areas not affected by desertification

Areas affected by desertification

Rainfed croplands 57 million ha.

Pattern of desertification

In the Sahel, desertification has been enhanced by human action. The diagram behind shows areas of bare ground around a settlement, caused by woodcutting for fuel, and around wells that have been bored down to water-bearing rocks ('aquifers').The diagram in front shows the same area after a well digging project. There has been no change in traditional herding practices, and more land has been overgrazed forming a larger bare area.

ATMOSPHERIC DUST	– makes the air more stable, reducing rainfall
ALBEDO CHANGES	– this is the change in the amount of sunlight a bare surface reflects in contrast to a vegetated surface. It may also reduce rainfall
SURFACE ROUGH-NESS CHANGES	– a bare soil surface presents less resistance to wind blowing over it. When large areas are laid bare this change may reduce rainfall.

Climatic feedback

Desertification over large areas may be having a significant effect on local climates. These three processes have been suggested as ways in which a changed natural surface can feedback on climate, further reducing rainfall.

17

7 Population

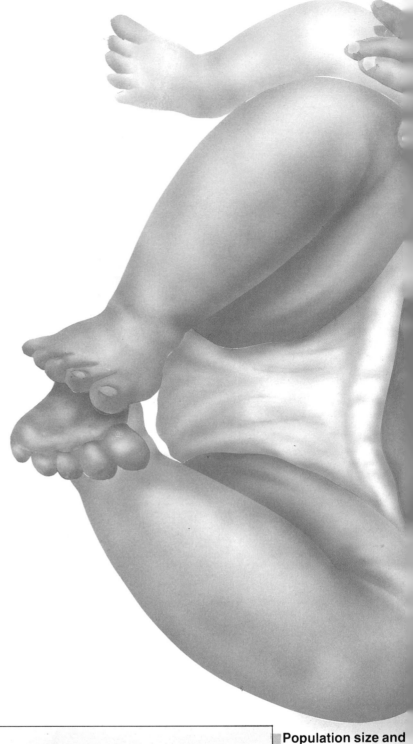

In 1986 there were over five billion people in the world. More than one billion live in China alone, the world's most populous country, and India has over 700 million inhabitants. The United Kingdom, by contrast, has a population of about 60 million. The most densely populated countries in the world are the small city states such as Hong Kong, where there is an average of 5,333 people per square kilometre.

A country's population structure is the number of males and females in different age groups. This structure is usually shown as a 'population pyramid' whose shape reflects a nation's population history (see below right).

The world's population is growing all the time. In most countries more people are born each year than die, population is also affected by people moving: migration. The population structure of developing countries in Africa, Asia and Latin America often shows many more young people than old. Since young people have babies, it is these countries that have experienced the world's population explosion.

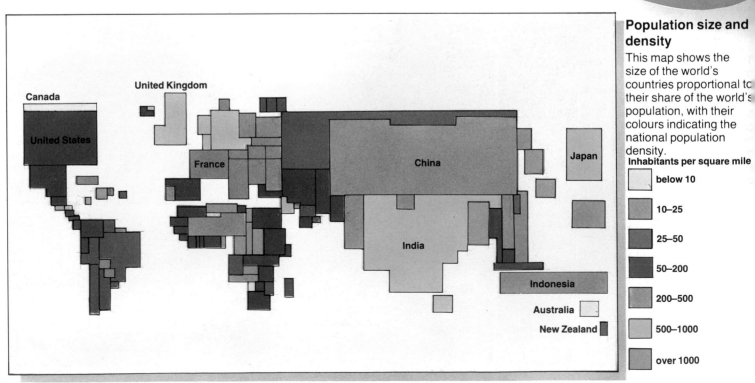

Population size and density

This map shows the size of the world's countries proportional to their share of the world's population, with their colours indicating the national population density.

Inhabitants per square mile

	below 10
	10–25
	25–50
	50–200
	200–500
	500–1000
	over 1000

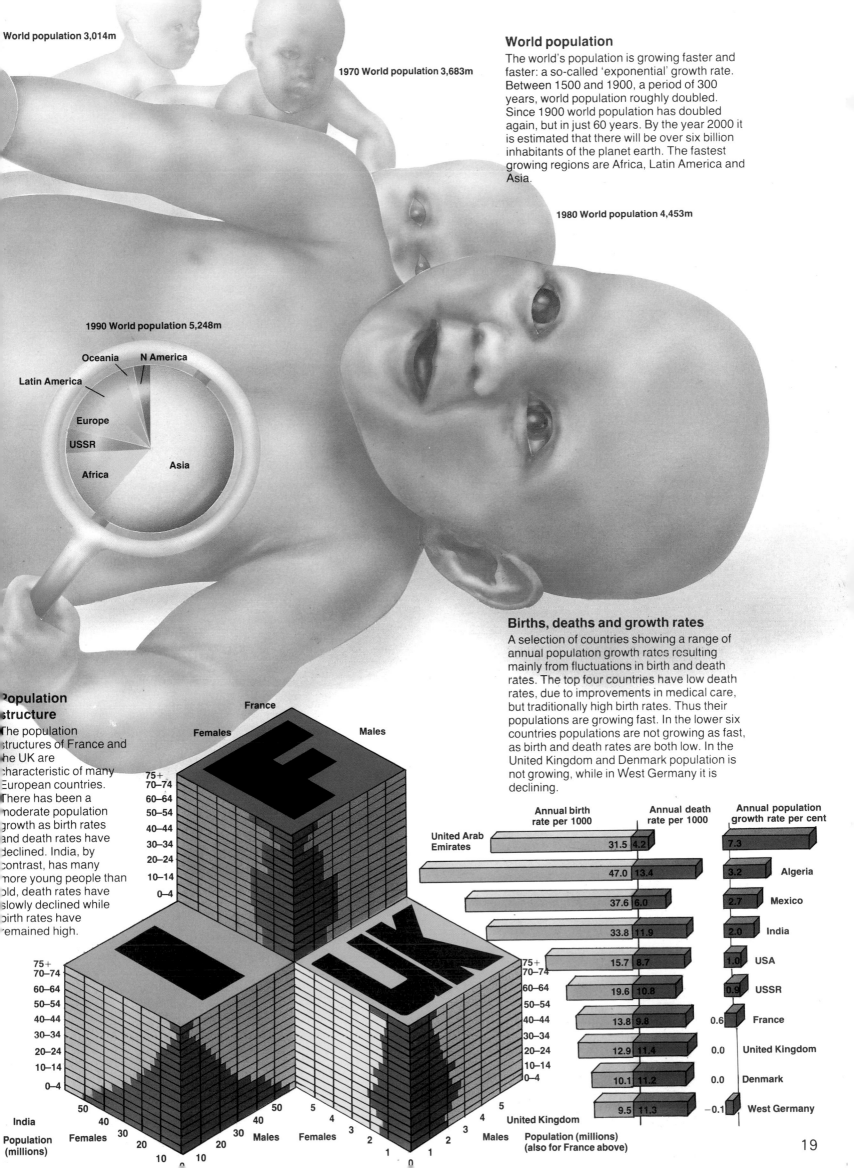

World population 3,014m

1970 World population 3,683m

1980 World population 4,453m

World population

The world's population is growing faster and faster: a so-called 'exponential' growth rate. Between 1500 and 1900, a period of 300 years, world population roughly doubled. Since 1900 world population has doubled again, but in just 60 years. By the year 2000 it is estimated that there will be over six billion inhabitants of the planet earth. The fastest growing regions are Africa, Latin America and Asia.

1990 World population 5,248m

Oceania
N America
Latin America
Europe
USSR
Africa
Asia

Births, deaths and growth rates

A selection of countries showing a range of annual population growth rates resulting mainly from fluctuations in birth and death rates. The top four countries have low death rates, due to improvements in medical care, but traditionally high birth rates. Thus their populations are growing fast. In the lower six countries populations are not growing as fast, as birth and death rates are both low. In the United Kingdom and Denmark population is not growing, while in West Germany it is declining.

Population structure

The population structures of France and the UK are characteristic of many European countries. There has been a moderate population growth as birth rates and death rates have declined. India, by contrast, has many more young people than old, death rates have slowly declined while birth rates have remained high.

France
Females   Males

	75+
	70–74
	60–64
	50–54
	40–44
	30–34
	20–24
	10–14
	0–4

India
Population (millions)
Females: 50 40 30 20 10
Males: 50 40 30 20 10

75+
70–74
60–64
50–54
40–44
30–34
20–24
10–14
0–4

UK
Females   Males
5 4 3 2 1   1 2 3 4 5

	Annual birth rate per 1000	Annual death rate per 1000	Annual population growth rate per cent
United Arab Emirates	31.5	4.2	7.3
Algeria	47.0	13.4	3.2
Mexico	37.6	6.0	2.7
India	33.8	11.9	2.0
USA	15.7	8.7	1.0
USSR	19.6	10.8	0.9
France	13.8	9.8	0.6
United Kingdom	12.9	11.4	0.0
Denmark	10.1	11.2	0.0
West Germany	9.5	11.3	-0.1

United Kingdom
Population (millions) (also for France above)

19

8 People & Places

The very large majority of the world's population lives in permanent settlements, be they village, towns or cities. In the countries of Europe, North America, Australia and Japan a high percentage of people live in cities or urban areas. In poorer countries, where a much larger proportion of the total population farms the land, the urban population is not so large.

As countries develop, their populations grow, and their economies become industrialised, so towns and cities expand. In Britain, Europe and the United States this growth of urban areas has slowed in recent years, but in some developing countries cities continue to grow at very fast rates.

These cities grow both in absorbing immigrants from the surrounding countryside who seek a better living, so-called 'rural-urban migration', and from the natural increase within cities that results from generally higher standards, lower death rates and better chances of a newborn child surviving.

Cities and shanties

One distressing aspect of Third World city growth is the development of 'shanty towns' on their outskirts. These are collections of makeshift shelters made from anything people can lay their hands on – corrugated iron, cardboard, tents. These shanty towns often lack water, electricity, roads and sanitation. One of the largest shanty towns is on the outskirts of Mexico City. It is called Netzhuacoyotl and has about 2 million inhabitants.

Migration

People move for many reasons. Migration is relatively permanent movement over quite large distances, so a walk to the local shops is not migration, neither is an hour's journey from home to work. Someone who leaves their country or region to settle in another country or region, however, is considered a migrant.

Reasons for migration may be 'push' or 'pull' factors. Push factors include lack of job opportunities, war and natural disasters; pull

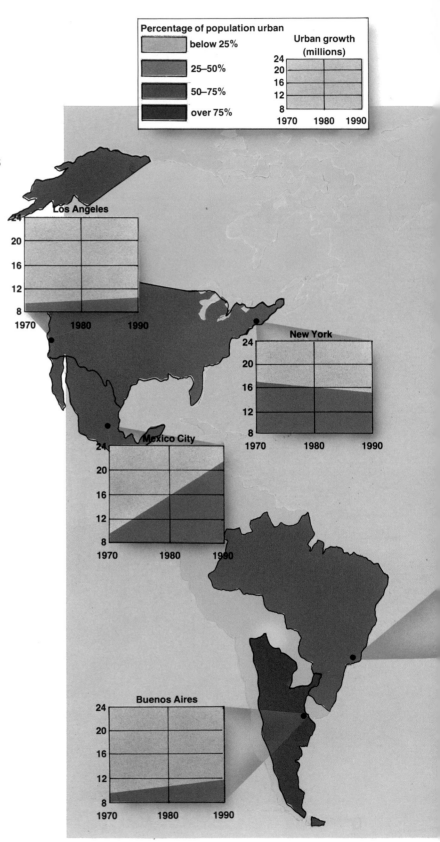

Percentage of population urban

below 25%

25–50%

50–75%

over 75%

Urban growth (millions)

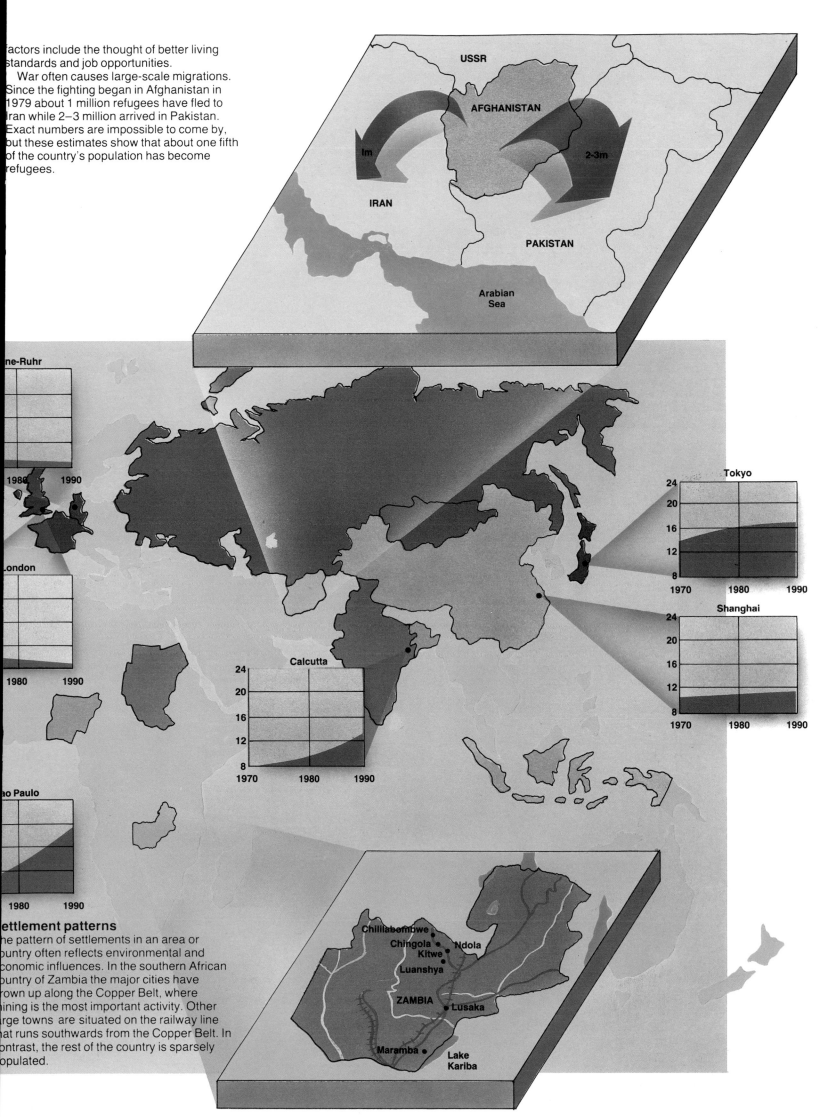

factors include the thought of better living standards and job opportunities.

War often causes large-scale migrations. Since the fighting began in Afghanistan in 1979 about 1 million refugees have fled to Iran while 2–3 million arrived in Pakistan. Exact numbers are impossible to come by, but these estimates show that about one fifth of the country's population has become refugees.

USSR

AFGHANISTAN

1m

IRAN

2-3m

PAKISTAN

Arabian Sea

Rhine-Ruhr

1980   1990

Tokyo

24
20
16
12
8

1970   1980   1990

London

1980   1990

Shanghai

24
20
16
12
8

1970   1980   1990

Calcutta

24
20
16
12
8

1970   1980   1990

São Paulo

1980   1990

Settlement patterns

The pattern of settlements in an area or country often reflects environmental and economic influences. In the southern African country of Zambia the major cities have grown up along the Copper Belt, where mining is the most important activity. Other large towns are situated on the railway line that runs southwards from the Copper Belt. In contrast, the rest of the country is sparsely populated.

Chililabombwe

Chingola   Ndola

Kitwe

Luanshya

ZAMBIA   Lusaka

Maramba

Lake Kariba

21

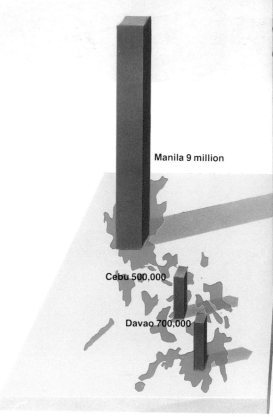

Water in

1,000 immigrants per day

Urbanization, the growth of cities, has increased at a fast rate this century. Whereas in 1900 about 14 per cent of the world's population lived in cities, today the figure is about 43 per cent. By the year 2000, if present growth rates continue, it will be more than half.

For most of this century the biggest cities in the world have been in the developed world, but now the cities of the Third World are becoming the largest, as we have seen in PEOPLE AND PLACES. At the present urban growth rate of 2.5 per cent yearly – half again as fast as the world population growth rate – the number of people living in cities throughout the world will double in the next 28 years.

Almost nine tenths of this growth will be in Third World cities, where the average urban growth rate is 3.5 per cent a year, more than three times the rate in developed countries. This growth is causing many problems of congestion in Third World cities, and at the same time making the problems of underdevelopment in rural areas worse.

Although many agree that Third World cities will continue to grow however, some experts consider that the rates of growth in the 1980s may be slower than in recent decades. Most Third World countries are experiencing economic difficulties and owe huge debts to international banks, and these problems may be reflected in a slowdown in urbanization rates when new census results become available.

Manila

Manila is a typical "primate" city, one that is very much larger than the second city and has a great concentration of the country's facilities. Although Manila has over 60 per cent of the Philippines' manufacturing industry, 16 per cent of the labour force is unemployed, since many of the factories use labour-saving machinery.

Living standards are low in Manila, with three fifths of all households living below the poverty line and just 11 per cent of the population served by sewers. Yet people are still attracted to the city; it is estimated that two thirds of all new housing is illegal and uncontrolled.

Manila 9 million

Cebu 500,000

Davao 700,000

Shanty towns

Uncontrolled, makeshift settlements are found on the edges of many third world cities. A number of different solutions have been tried by governments to solve this problem, although most developing countries do nothing through a lack of money.

Bulldozing

For example in South Africa, but this often leads to unrest.

Mass Rehousing Projects

For example in Nigeria in the 1970s, but even in oil-rich countries this is too expensive to solve the whole problem.

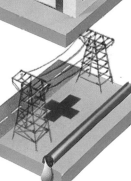

Improving Settlements

For example in Lusaka, Zambia in the late 1970s. Building of roads, providing water, electricity, and health services.

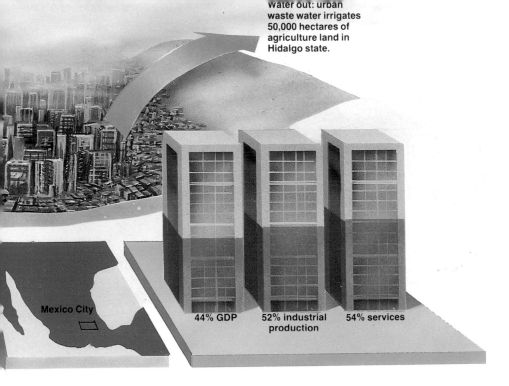

Water out: urban waste water irrigates 50,000 hectares of agriculture land in Hidalgo state.

Mexico City

44% GDP   52% industrial production   54% services

Mexico City

Mexico City is probably the world's largest city, with a population of between 18 and 19 million, about 22 per cent of Mexico's population. It is by far the most important commercial, industrial, political and transportational centre in the country. Mexico City produces no less than 44 per cent of Mexico's GDP, 52 per cent of all industrial production and has 54 per cent of the nation's services.

The city was first built on a series of lakes in the Valley of Mexico some 2,500 metres above sea level. Today almost all the lakes have gone dry, and water for the city's people and industry is pumped from a site over 100 km away and 1,000 metres lower. In the 1990s more water will have to be pumped from another site, 200 km away and 2,000 m lower. This will need six new power stations to do the pumping.

Despite the overcrowding and the growing "shanty city" of Netzhaucoyotl, over 1,000 people a day arrive in Mexico City to make it their home. Many do not find jobs. Pollution is so bad in Mexico City that breathing the air is said to be the same as smoking 40 cigarettes a day.

Sao Paulo

1930
population: 1 million
area: 150 sq km

1962   population: 4 million   area: 750 sq km

1980   population: 12 million   area: 1400 sq km

Sao Paulo

Brazil's largest city and, after Mexico City, the second largest in Latin America, Sao Paulo has expanded at an alarming rate this century. The city has been given large amounts of government money, to the neglect of much of the rest of Brazil. In 1975, Sao Paulo had less than 10 per cent of the country's population but consumed 44 per cent of Brazil's electricity, had 39 per cent of all telephones and more than half the industrial output and employment.

Every day Sao Paulo's industry and motor vehicles pour more than 8,000 tonnes of pollution into the city's air, causing an increase in mortality among infants and people over 65 years old.

10 Food & Water

It is estimated that about 30 per cent of the world's land area can be cultivated. The rest is either too cold, too dry, too steep or otherwise unsuitable. Of the land being cultivated about half is actually used for growing crops. The remainder is pasture, meadowland or forest.

The types of food produced in different parts of the world reflect the world's differing climates and types of soil. Rice cultivation, for example, requires lots of water and a hot climate so that it is typically grown in tropical, rainy climates. Cereal crops, on the other hand, such as wheat, thrive in more temperate climates where there is less rain and enough sun to ripen the crop.

The oceans offer vast food resources. Fish are especially high in protein, a lack of which is the most serious problem for most of the world's undernourished population. Japan, which has little farmland, is the largest single consumer of fish. In 1983 Japanese fleets caught more fish than all of western Europe combined.

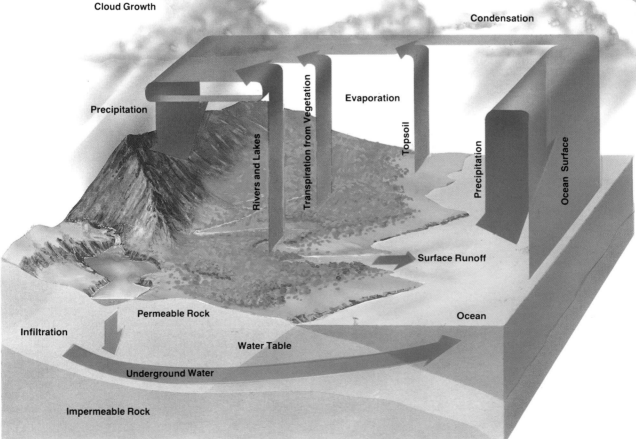

Cloud Growth

Condensation

Precipitation

Transpiration from Vegetation

Evaporation

Rivers and Lakes

Topsoil

Precipitation

Ocean Surface

Surface Runoff

Permeable Rock

Ocean

Infiltration

Water Table

Underground Water

Impermeable Rock

The Hydrological Cycle

Water is essential to life on earth. The total amount of water in the oceans, in the atmosphere, on the land and in the soil is constant, but it is continually being recycled. Water from the sea, rivers and lakes, vegetation and the soil is put into the atmosphere. As it cools the water condenses or freezes and falls as rain, hail or snow over the land or sea. Some of this water soaks into the soil, some is used by vegetation, some flows back into the sea, while some evaporates again directly into the air.

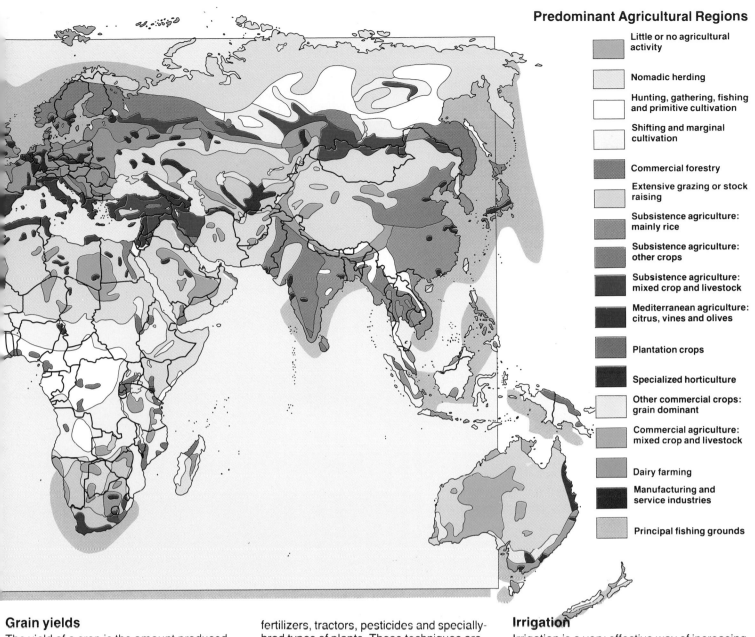

Predominant Agricultural Regions

- Little or no agricultural activity
- Nomadic herding
- Hunting, gathering, fishing and primitive cultivation
- Shifting and marginal cultivation
- Commercial forestry
- Extensive grazing or stock raising
- Subsistence agriculture: mainly rice
- Subsistence agriculture: other crops
- Subsistence agriculture: mixed crop and livestock
- Mediterranean agriculture: citrus, vines and olives
- Plantation crops
- Specialized horticulture
- Other commercial crops: grain dominant
- Commercial agriculture: mixed crop and livestock
- Dairy farming
- Manufacturing and service industries
- Principal fishing grounds

Grain yields

The yield of a crop is the amount produced from a standard area of field. The diagram shows that the grain yields from western Europe and the United States are more than four times those from Africa. This is because developed world agriculture uses more fertilizers, tractors, pesticides and specially-bred types of plants. These techniques are expensive. Developing countries do not have as much money to train farmers in these methods, or to buy fertilizers. Ploughs are more often pulled by animals rather than by tractors in these countries.

Grain yields by region (kg per hectare)

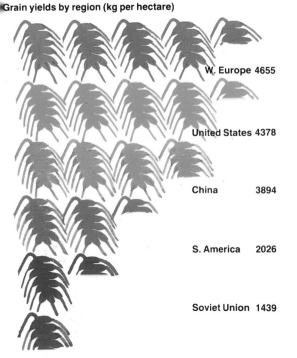

W. Europe	4655
United States	4378
China	3894
S. America	2026
Soviet Union	1439
Africa	890

A % cultivated land under irrigation
B % total food production from irrigated land

Irrigation

Irrigation is a very effective way of increasing crop yields. Water for irrigation can be taken from rivers, sometimes stored in dams until needed, or from water-holding rocks deep below the ground surface.

Irrigation is expensive however. Canals and sprinklers need constant maintenance and careful management since too much water put on to the land may ruin the crops by waterlogging or a build-up of salts.

A

Peru	India	China	Pakistan	Indonesia
35	30	50	65	

B

Peru	India	China	Pakistan	Indonesia
40	55	55	70	80	50

11 Agricultural Systems

There are four basic types of farming systems, based on the sort of cultivation used (see right). The first is concerned with 'perennial' trees or vines, such as used in orchards, vineyards or rubber plantations. The second approach is based on cultivated crops, such as corn or wheat, which are replanted in freshly tilled soil after the harvest. The third system involves grazing of permanent grasslands, and the fourth alternates cultivated crops with grass or some other crop used to feed animals.

The type of farming system used in any area depends upon many factors, including the climate and soils of the region and the influences of local and international markets if the agricultural produce is to be sold.

There are many differences between the agricultural practices used in the world's developed countries and those in the poorer nations, quite apart from those due to differences in climate and soils. Farmers in the developed world use machines and many types of fertilizers and pesticides. The use of these techniques has produced much greater yields from fields (see FOOD AND WATER), and thus these techniques are being adopted by many Third World countries. Such adoption is not always possible or even successful however. Machines and chemicals are expensive and farmers need to be trained to use them effectively. Machines also need maintenance, fuel and spare parts that are not always easy to obtain.

Crop production in the United States
The US government has encouraged their farmers to grow as much as possible of the major crops (wheat, soya beans, and the feed grains: corn, sorghum, barley and oats). The result has been better yields per hectare, an increase in national production and an increase in planted area. This better productivity has been gained by more payments to farmers, allowing them to use better machinery and more chemicals on the land.

However, this policy has often meant more erosion, as unsuitable land is planted, and worries about the serious effects of chemical fertilizers and pesticides in polluting the environment.

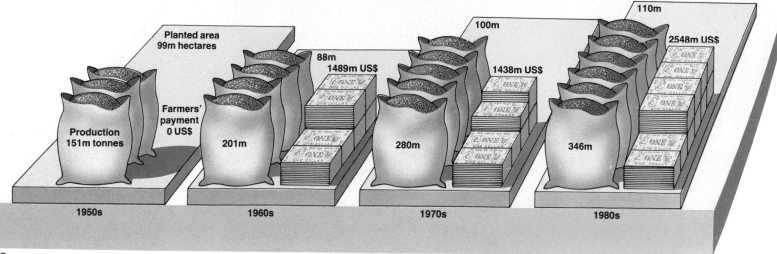

1950s
Planted area 99m hectares
Production 151m tonnes
Farmers' payment 0 US$

1960s
88m
1489m US$
201m

1970s
100m
1438m US$
280m

1980s
110m
2548m US$
346m

Crop production in Africa

In Africa, as in other countries, some crops are grown for local people's use, others for export. The crops that are sold are known as 'cash crops'. One reason some suggest for the African Food Crisis of the early 1980s (see FAMINE AND PLENTY) is that the growing of cash crops for export has expanded at the expense of home food production. This has not happened, but in some areas where cash crops for export have been expanded it has occurred onto land that once grew food and food production has been pushed onto poorer land (see West Volta project below).

Burkina Faso: West Volta project

Burkina Faso's production of cotton for export rose from 2,000 tonnes in 1960 to 75,000 tonnes in 1984. Much of this increase has come from the West Volta project in the south of the country where annual rainfall is 1,000 mm or more. The cotton is 'rainfed', which means that no irrigation is used, and the yields of 1,000 kg per hectare are twice those for Africa south of the Sahara as a whole. Fertilizers are used, but the emphasis is on methods that village farmers can easily employ.

The West Volta project is in an area with good soils, enough reliable rain and adequate transport. Traditional agriculture is the cultivation of millet and sorghum by ox and hand ploughing and, on the desert margin, nomadic cattle herding. Since the 1960s food production, in contrast to cotton production, has remained stable.

Nigeria: alley cropping

One answer to the problems of farming in humid areas has been developed in Nigeria, and is known as 'alley cropping.' Crops such as yams are grown in strips or alleys between rows of trees. The trees are 'leguminous', which means that they are good at allowing nitrogen to be made in the soil, a mineral essential to plant growth. Leguminous plants include peas and beans.

There are many advantages to alley cropping. The trees are pruned and their leaves spread on the alleys to improve the soil, so that expensive fertilizers are not needed. Extra leaves can be fed to animals and wood from the trees is used as fuel. The trees also protect the alley crops from erosion. Perhaps most importantly alley cropping means that land can be used continuously, producing yields of two tonnes per hectare without fertilizer (more than double the Nigerian average). Traditional methods meant that plots had to be left unused for a few years after cultivation for the soil to recover its goodness.

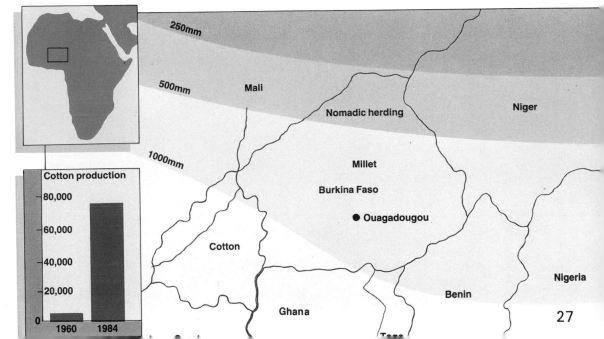

12 Famine & Plenty

The earth produces enough food to feed its present population. In North America and Europe, however, too much food is produced, whereas in many poorer countries there is not enough.

The worst irony of the bad distribution of food is that large amounts are stored as 'mountains' in Europe for example where there is too much food produced. At the same time people in Africa may be starving because they do not have enough to eat. The solution to the problem is not always straightforward though, since in some parts of the world people do not eat the same types of food as we do in Europe (bottom right).

One of the consequences of food availability is shown over the page. Someone who eats too much of the wrong foods is likely to die earlier because of it. In other countries people may die because they cannot find enough to keep them alive. In this country many people go on special diets to become thinner because they like to be thin. In India, by contrast, rich people prefer to be fat because it is a sign that they have enough to eat.

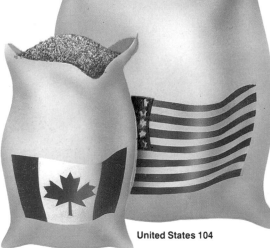

2690

2520

2520

2640

2390

Grain for sale

The various types of grain, such as wheat, maize and rice, are the most important food source for almost everyone. These are the countries that grow enough grain for their own populations and still have large amounts for export. The dominance of the United States in world grain exports is clear. For some countries, importing US grain is useful because they cannot grow enough of their own, but at the same time the incentive for such countries to produce more at home is not so great if they can import easily from elsewhere.

The main importers of grain are the Soviet Union and the African countries. In the last ten years both have been importing more and more. Soviet grain production is inefficient; much grain is lost in storage and during transport. In Africa, many countries have not produced enough to feed themselves because of drought. Also in Africa the growing of cash crops (see AGRICULTURAL SYSTEMS) has often meant that less emphasis is put on producing grain to feed their people.

Principal grain exporters
(million tonnes)

United Kingdom 6   Thailand 8   Australia 15   Argentina 17   France 25   Canada 27   United States 104

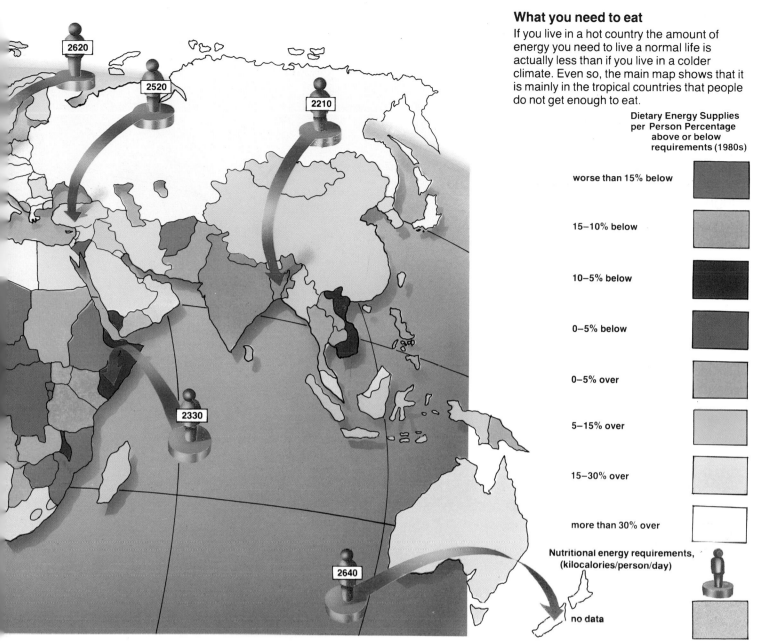

What you need to eat

If you live in a hot country the amount of energy you need to live a normal life is actually less than if you live in a colder climate. Even so, the main map shows that it is mainly in the tropical countries that people do not get enough to eat.

Dietary Energy Supplies per Person Percentage above or below requirements (1980s)

worse than 15% below	
15–10% below	
10–5% below	
0–5% below	
0–5% over	
5–15% over	
15–30% over	
more than 30% over	

Nutritional energy requirements, (kilocalories/person/day)

no data

ood not eaten

hese are areas of the orld where certain pes of food are not aten by the local eople. Usually such voidance is for ligious reasons. For xample, pork is not aten by Muslims or ews.

Pork	
Beef	
Chicken and/or eggs	
Milk products	

13 Healthy & Wealthy

The average age to which a person is expected to live, their 'life expectancy', varies dramatically according to where that person lives. If you are born and live in Afghanistan, for example, you can expect to live until you are 37. If you live in Japan you will probably survive until you are over 70. Many factors are involved, but if you live in a rich country you can reasonably expect to live longer than someone in a poorer country.

One of the important influences on life expectancy is the chance of a new-born baby living beyond its first birthday. This is known as the 'infant mortality rate' (see right). In most European countries less than 20 babies per 1000 die before their first birthday. In much of Africa the figure is over 100.

Although many poor tropical countries suffer from diseases that are very hard to prevent, infant mortality and life expectancy could be greatly improved by simple measures. Among these measures is the provision of things people in Europe and North America often take for granted, such as clean water and sanitation.

Drinking water and sanitation

In 1983 the World Health Organisation estimated that half of the people in developing countries could not easily get safe drinking water. Three out of every four people in these countries had no kind of sanitary facilities, not even a bucket or a pit.

Water can carry disease. Every day, throughout the world, about 25,000 people die from diseases related to dirty water.

Within developing countries the situation is usually worst in the countryside. In the East African state of Tanzania, for example, only 28 per cent of rural people have access to safe drinking water, compared to 82 per cent in the capital Dar-es-Salaam.

Population per doctor

The large differences in the number of doctors available to treat the people of various countries can be seen immediately. In some parts of the world, however, there are also other traditional doctors such as acupuncturists, particularly in China, and herbalists. Within the poorer countries the lack of health care is worse in rural areas because often the doctors and hospitals are concentrated in the big cities.

Western Europe
476

USA
549

USSR
248

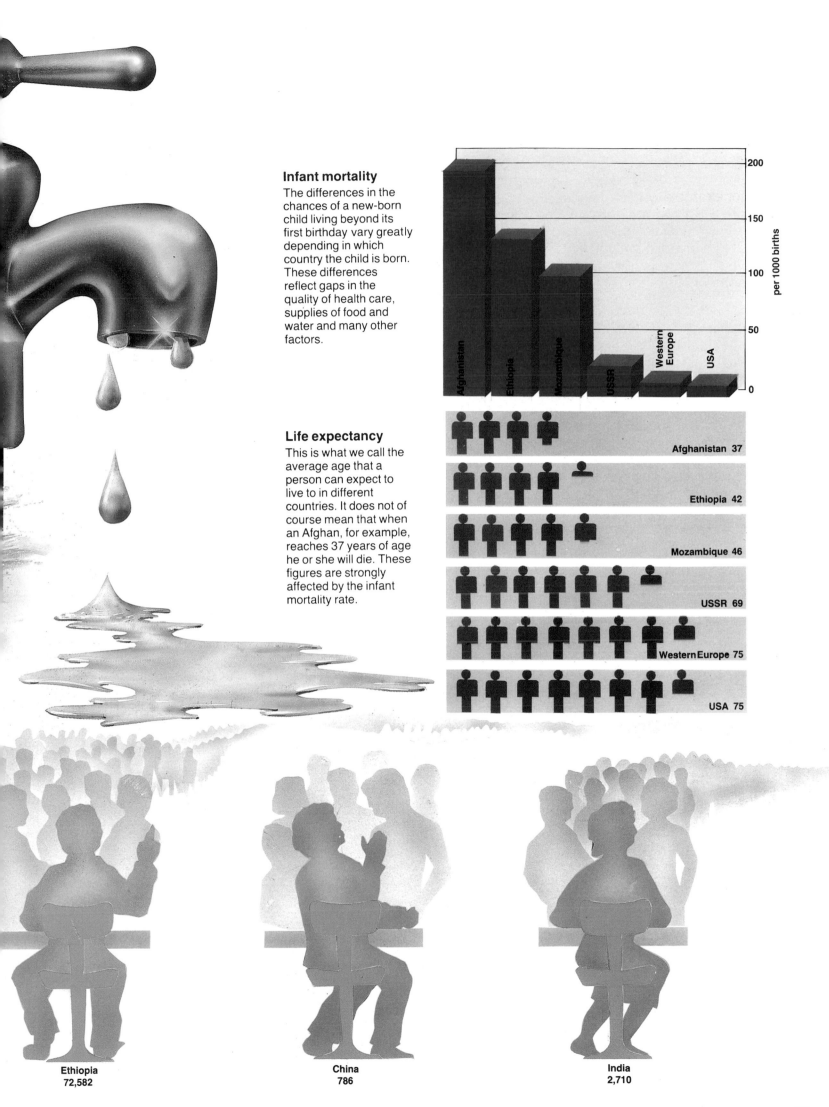

Infant mortality

The differences in the chances of a new-born child living beyond its first birthday vary greatly depending in which country the child is born. These differences reflect gaps in the quality of health care, supplies of food and water and many other factors.

per 1000 births

Afghanistan

Ethiopia

Mozambique

USSR

Western Europe

USA

Life expectancy

This is what we call the average age that a person can expect to live to in different countries. It does not of course mean that when an Afghan, for example, reaches 37 years of age he or she will die. These figures are strongly affected by the infant mortality rate.

Afghanistan 37

Ethiopia 42

Mozambique 46

USSR 69

Western Europe 75

USA 75

Ethiopia
72,582

China
786

India
2,710

14 Diseased & Dying

Many people in the developing countries never live to a 'ripe old age'. The reasons for this are linked to poverty, and could be prevented. They include undernourishment, contaminated water, lack of sanitation and medical care, and lack of education.

In the countries of Europe and North America, people commonly die of diseases caused by eating food that is too rich, a lack of exercise and smoking. Heart diseases and cancer are the most frequent killers. The fact that people tend to live longer in these countries also means that diseases of old age are more common than in other nations.

By contrast, the most prevalent causes of death in Africa, Asia and Latin America are diseases such as diarrhoea. Children are the main victims. Other ailments that also mainly affect children include measles, whooping cough, polio and tetanus. In the United Kingdom most children are immunised against these, in poorer countries the children are not always so lucky.

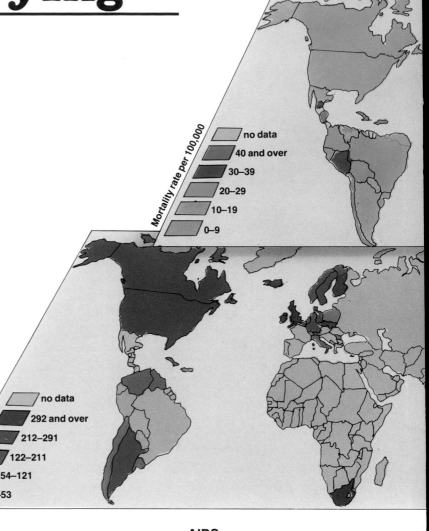

Mortality rate per 100,000
- no data
- 40 and over
- 30–39
- 20–29
- 10–19
- 0–9

Mortality rate per 100,000
- no data
- 292 and over
- 212–291
- 122–211
- 54–121
- 1–53

Uganda
Congo
Zaire
Rwanda
Burundi
Kenya
Tanzania
Zambia

AIDS

This is a new disease which is claiming victims in many countries of the world. The situation is worst in the central African nations shown. Although the numbers of casualties are not large on a world scale, the disease is spreading fast. The search is on for a cure before the situation gets out of hand. At the start of 1988 there were 1200 AIDS cases in Britain. At that time 697 people had died from the disease.

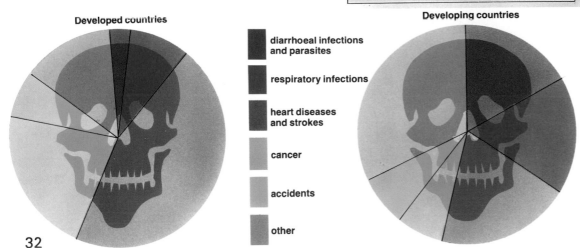

Developed countries

Developing countries

- diarrhoeal infections and parasites
- respiratory infections
- heart diseases and strokes
- cancer
- accidents
- other

Cause of death

A comparison of the relative importance of causes of death in developed and developing countries.

Bronchitis

A respiratory disease which can particularly affect smokers.

Malaria and Yellow Fever

These tropical diseases are spread by mosquitoes that breed in stagnant water.

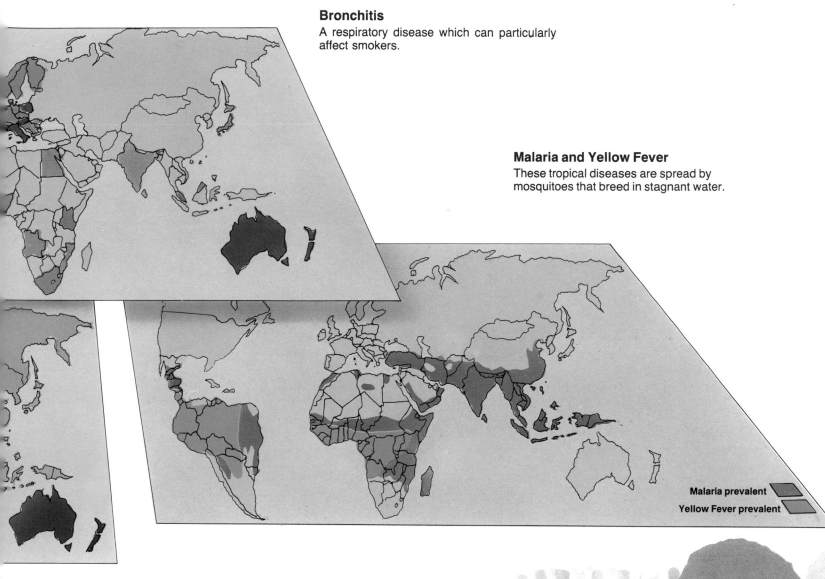

Malaria prevalent

Yellow Fever prevalent

Heart disease

Information for many of the world's developing countries is difficult to obtain, but the rich diets of the developed countries make people more likely to suffer from heart disease.

Immunisation

People can be protected against many diseases by immunisation, and over time the disease may disappear. Smallpox, which used to be a major world killer, was completely wiped out in 1980.

Preventable child-killing diseases

The major diseases of childhood are diptheria, whooping cough, tetanus, polio, measles and tuberculosis. All these are preventable by vaccination. In the developed countries these diseases have been greatly reduced by vaccination programmes, improvements in housing, nutrition and public health. However, they continue to kill or disable several million children each year in developing countries. The annual number of deaths from some of these diseases are shown here for a selection of Third World nations.

Number of deaths from selected vaccine-preventable diseases.

	Tetanus	Measles	Whooping Cough
India	98,000	82,000	89,000
Indonesia	71,000	218,000	63,000
Nigeria	64,000	171,000	68,000
Mexico	31,000	57,000	19,000
Brazil	28,000	34,000	18,000
Vietnam	10,000	57,000	11,000

15 Mineral Resources

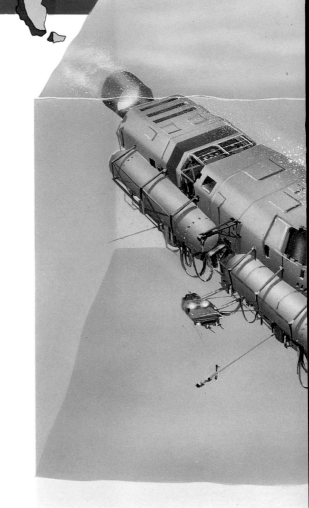

Minerals are vitally important to every society. They are all around us. There are minerals in the food we eat, the water we drink, and the things we use.

Many of the minerals found in rocks are useful metals. Iron is the most widely used, which when other minerals are added, is made into steel. For example, if tungsten is added the steel is hard, if a magnetic steel is needed cobalt is added, and the strongest steels are made with manganese.

Gold is the most precious metal. Most countries keep large quantities in their bank vaults because it never loses its value and everybody seems to want it.

The world distribution of minerals is uneven. The biggest countries, such as the Soviet Union, China, the United States and Brazil have good supplies of many minerals. The United Kingdom does not produce large quantities of any important minerals (except fuels, see ENERGY). The small Caribbean island of Jamaica, however, is an important world producer of bauxite, which is used to make aluminium.

World mineral reserves

The dates of exhaustion can only be very rough. More reserves may be discovered, greater proportions can be obtained by recycling and alternatives can be found.

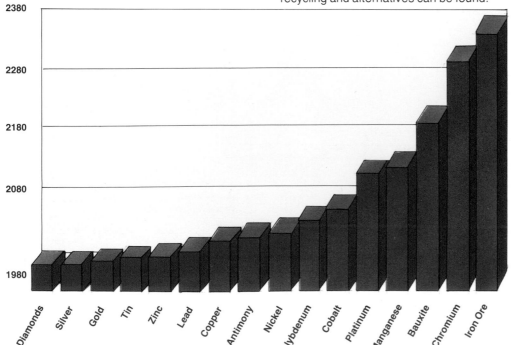

Year of exhaustion

Diamonds · Silver · Gold · Tin · Zinc · Lead · Copper · Antimony · Nickel · Molybdenum · Cobalt · Platinum · Manganese · Bauxite · Chromium · Iron Ore

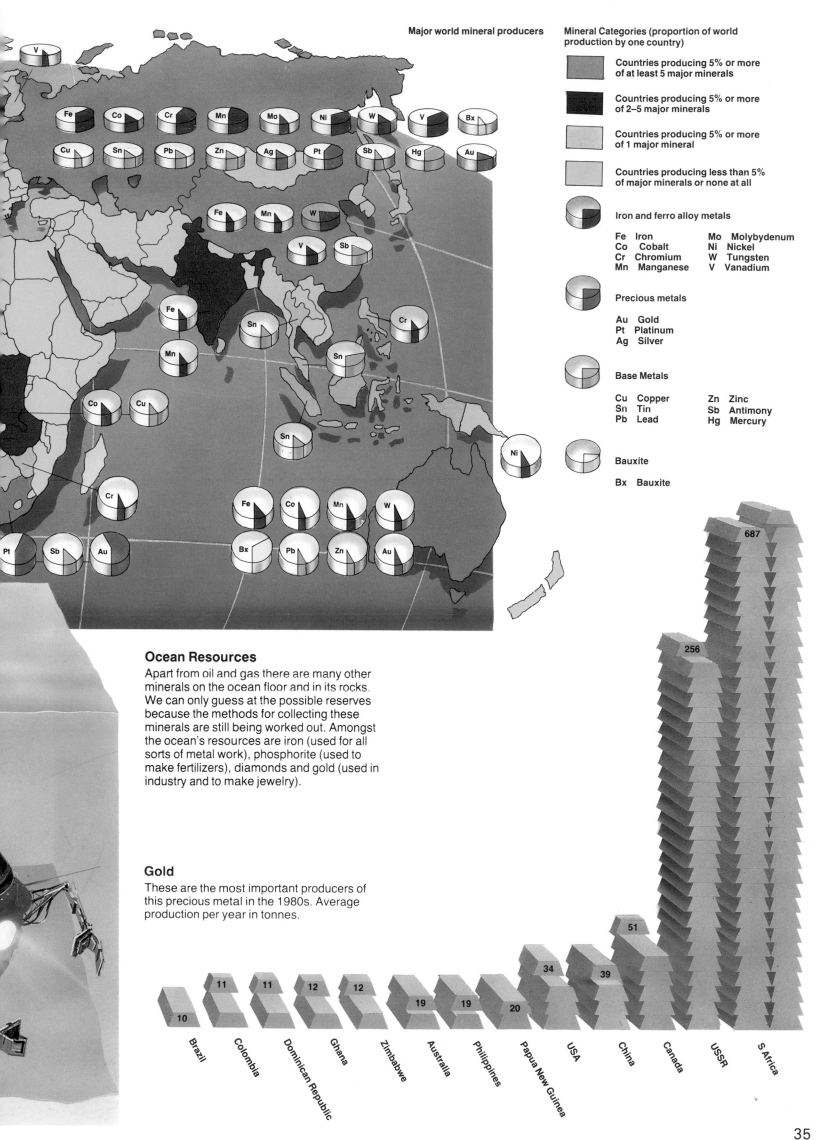

Major world mineral producers

Mineral Categories (proportion of world production by one country)

Countries producing 5% or more of at least 5 major minerals

Countries producing 5% or more of 2–5 major minerals

Countries producing 5% or more of 1 major mineral

Countries producing less than 5% of major minerals or none at all

Iron and ferro alloy metals

Fe	Iron	Mo	Molybdenum
Co	Cobalt	Ni	Nickel
Cr	Chromium	W	Tungsten
Mn	Manganese	V	Vanadium

Precious metals

Au Gold
Pt Platinum
Ag Silver

Base Metals

Cu	Copper	Zn	Zinc
Sn	Tin	Sb	Antimony
Pb	Lead	Hg	Mercury

Bauxite

Bx Bauxite

Ocean Resources

Apart from oil and gas there are many other minerals on the ocean floor and in its rocks. We can only guess at the possible reserves because the methods for collecting these minerals are still being worked out. Amongst the ocean's resources are iron (used for all sorts of metal work), phosphorite (used to make fertilizers), diamonds and gold (used in industry and to make jewelry).

Gold

These are the most important producers of this precious metal in the 1980s. Average production per year in tonnes.

Brazil 10
Colombia 11
Dominican Republic 11
Ghana 12
Zimbabwe 12
Australia 19
Philippines 19
Papua New Guinea 20
USA 34
China 39
Canada 51
USSR 256
S Africa 687

16 Energy

Energy is vital to practically every human activity, from cooking the breakfast to building a space rocket. Almost the entire world supply of commercial energy is from 'fossil fuels' : coal, oil and natural gas. These are the products of vegetation that was alive millions of years ago and has been changed as it has become part of the earth's rocks.

These fossil fuels will not last for ever. It is estimated that oil may last for another 30 years, coal for 250 years. At present just four per cent of commercial energy is generated by other methods. Special local conditions are needed for hydro-electricity, geothermal power, wind power, solar power and tidal power, but nuclear energy is the most obvious power source to expand. There are terrifying hazards with this form of energy, however, as shown by the fire at the Chernobyl reactor in the Soviet Union in 1986.

The map does not show all the energy used in the world. About 15 per cent is produced for very local use, mainly from burning wood. This is the main energy source for about two billion people, most of them in the Third World. Although wood should be a renewable energy source, in some areas trees and shrubs are being cut down faster than new plants can grow, causing a severe shortage (see VEGETATION).

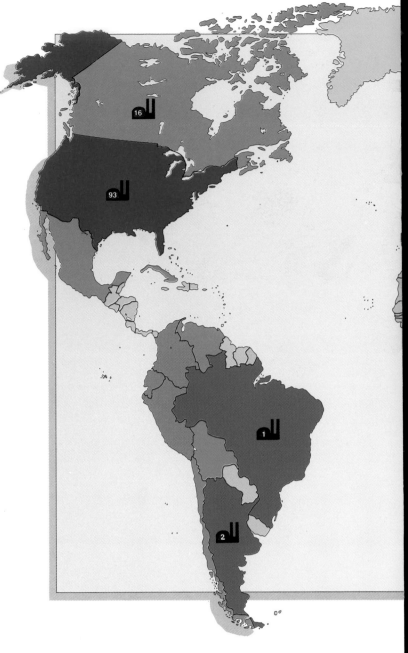

Oil trade
The world's largest source of energy is oil. Here the ten biggest oil exporters are shown with their main customers. Notice that the five

Consumption and production
The world's ten largest energy consumers compared with their production.

million tonnes coal equivalent

surplus

deficit

production / consumption

consumption / production

USA   USSR   China   Japan   W Germany   UK   Canada   France   Italy   India

2000   1600   1500   1000   600   500   400   300   200   100   0

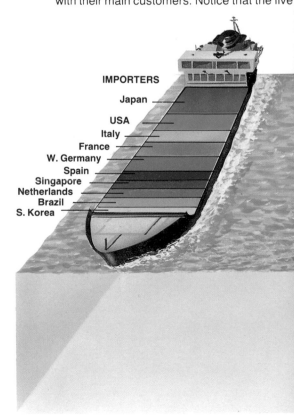

IMPORTERS

Japan
USA
Italy
France
W. Germany
Spain
Singapore
Netherlands
Brazil
S. Korea

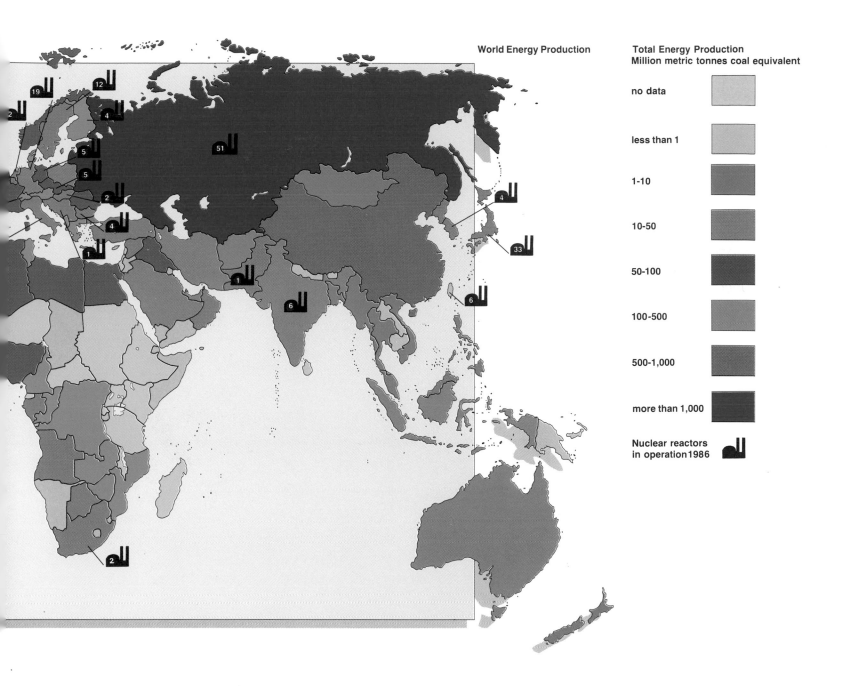

World Energy Production

Total Energy Production
Million metric tonnes coal equivalent

no data

less than 1

1-10

10-50

50-100

100-500

500-1,000

more than 1,000

Nuclear reactors
in operation 1986

largest importers of oil are among the top ten energy consumers, the countries who do not produce enough of their own energy (those with red flames in the diagram left).

Nuclear power in Europe

Most of the nuclear power stations are in Europe (see map). This diagram shows the importance of nuclear power generation in eight European countries as a percentage of all power generated.

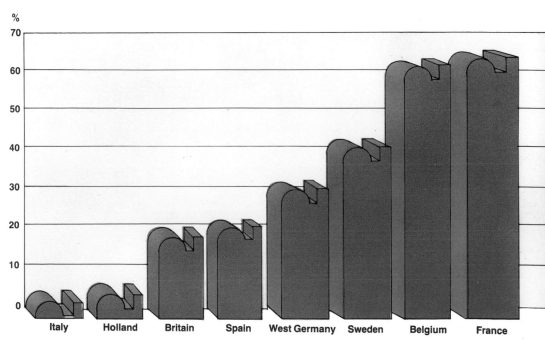

EXPORTERS
Saudi Arabia
Mexico
Iran
Indonesia
UK
UAE
Libya
Iraq
Nigeria
Venezuela

%

Italy | Holland | Britain | Spain | West Germany | Sweden | Belgium | France

17 Industry

A successful manufacturing industry is generally thought to be the basis for a prosperous country's economy. A nation's industry can sell its products to its own people, the 'domestic market', and if the products are of good quality they can be sold to other countries. In western Europe, North America and Japan manufacturing industry is well developed, and products from these countries are sold all over the world.

Developing countries with large populations, such as India and Brazil, have ready domestic markets for their goods, but other developing countries find it difficult to build their industry because selling their products on the world market is not easy. Many of these countries are dependent on selling 'raw materials' (either agricultural or mineral) that are processed in developed countries.

In North America and western Europe manufacturing industry is not as important as it was 30 years ago. During this time 'service industries' have expanded rapidly. These are organisations that offer a service to society, such as banking, tourism and insurance, rather than made products. In eastern Europe, however, manufacturing is still the most important part of the economy, most of their products being for their own countries. (Compare the proportions of people employed in different occupations in A JOB OF WORK).

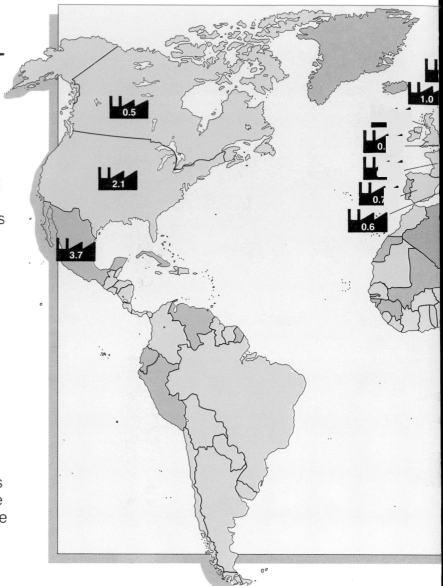

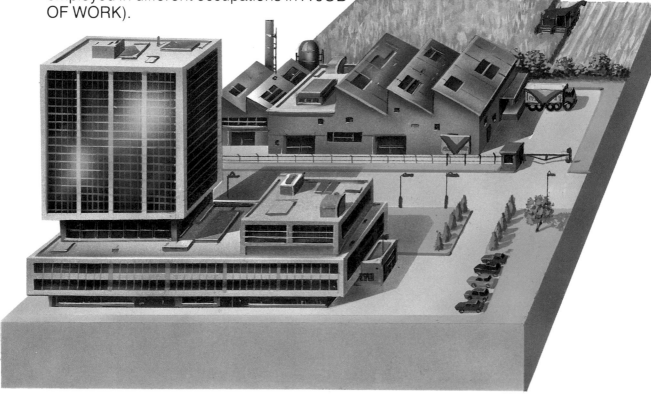

Three types of indust
Industry is usually divided into three:

Primary Industry
includes fishing, forestry, mining, quarrying, hunting and agriculture.

Secondary Industry
includes all manufacturing.

Tertiary Industry
includes all services.

Usually when we speak of industrial nations we mean manufacturing nations.

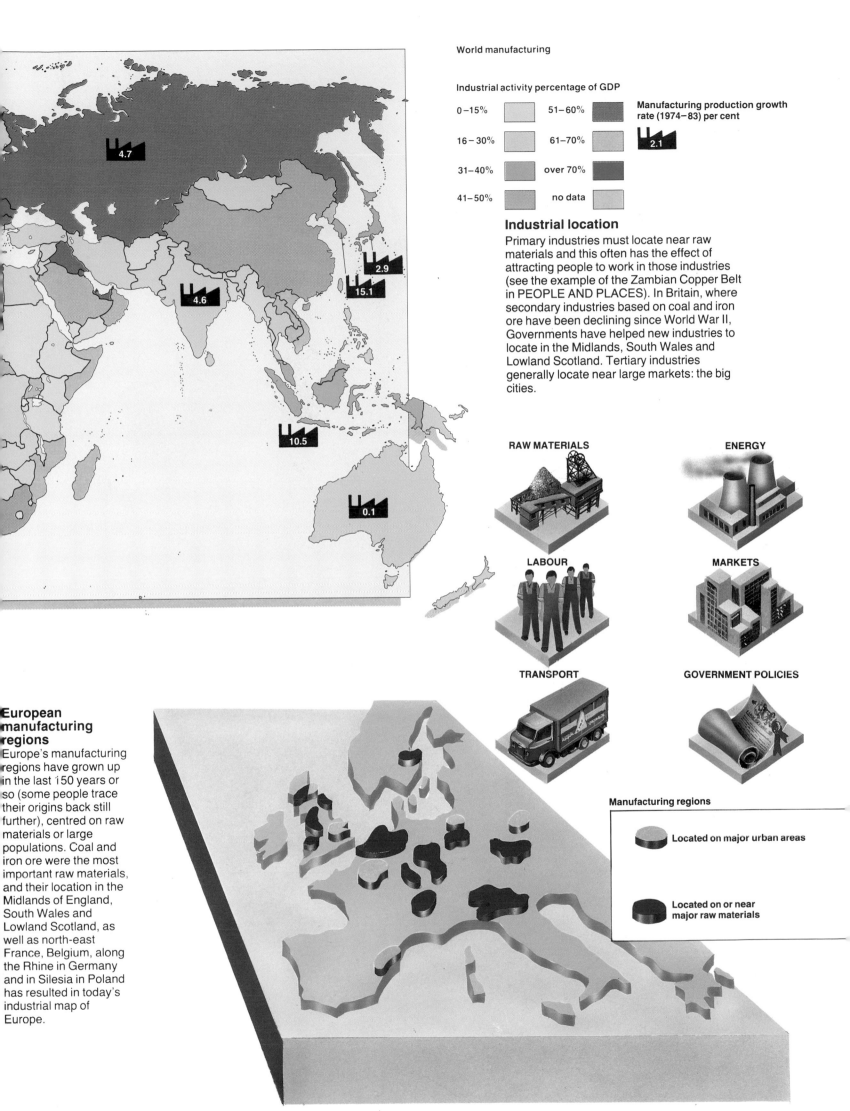

World manufacturing

Industrial activity percentage of GDP

0–15%		51–60%	
16–30%		61–70%	
31–40%		over 70%	
41–50%		no data	

Manufacturing production growth rate (1974–83) per cent

2.1

4.7

2.9

4.6

15.1

10.5

0.1

Industrial location

Primary industries must locate near raw materials and this often has the effect of attracting people to work in those industries (see the example of the Zambian Copper Belt in PEOPLE AND PLACES). In Britain, where secondary industries based on coal and iron ore have been declining since World War II, Governments have helped new industries to locate in the Midlands, South Wales and Lowland Scotland. Tertiary industries generally locate near large markets: the big cities.

RAW MATERIALS

ENERGY

LABOUR

MARKETS

TRANSPORT

GOVERNMENT POLICIES

European manufacturing regions

Europe's manufacturing regions have grown up in the last 150 years or so (some people trace their origins back still further), centred on raw materials or large populations. Coal and iron ore were the most important raw materials, and their location in the Midlands of England, South Wales and Lowland Scotland, as well as north-east France, Belgium, along the Rhine in Germany and in Silesia in Poland has resulted in today's industrial map of Europe.

Manufacturing regions

Located on major urban areas

Located on or near major raw materials

18 A Job of Work

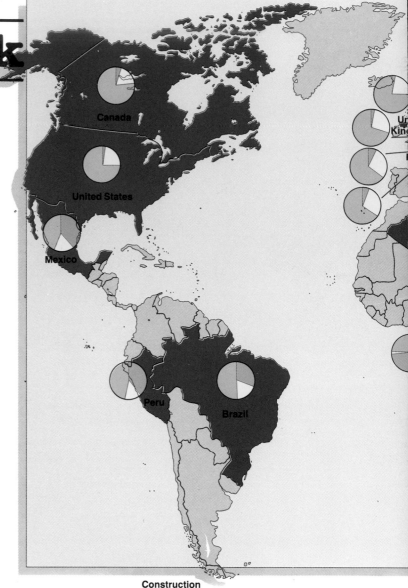

There are three basic categories of employment: people may work in either the primary, secondary or tertiary industries (see INDUSTRY). The proportions of the national work-force employed in each of these sectors is an indicator of a country's development.

In the early stages of development the majority of the work-force work in the primary sector, mostly as farmers, but also in mining. This was the case in the United Kingdom before the industrial revolution, and is still the situation in many of today's developing countries (see map).

As industry develops more people are employed in factories (see the Soviet Union on the map), and gradually the service sector takes over as the largest employer (see the United States, United Kingdom and France on the map).

Unemployment is one of the disturbing problems that modern governments are having to face. In developed countries people without jobs are paid a living wage by their government, but in developing countries there is often no such Social Security system. Hence many people in Third World cities are forced to beg for a living.

Peru

Of a total population of about 19 million, this South American country has a work-force of 6 million. Further breakdown of the work-force into employment categories shows the dominant importance of primary industry. The 28 percent in "services and others" includes the large numbers who work in the informal service sector (see right).

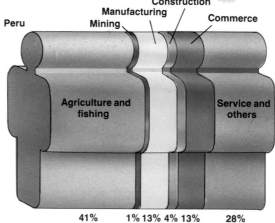

Peru

Mining · Manufacturing · Construction · Commerce

Agriculture and fishing · Service and others

41%   1% 13% 4% 13%   28%

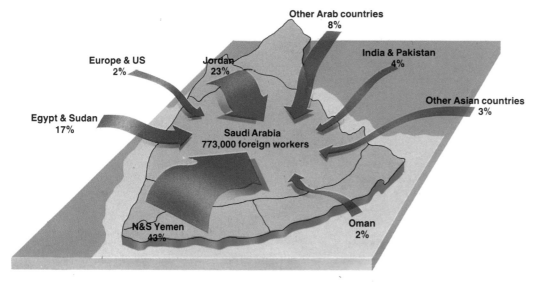

Other Arab countries 8%

Europe & US 2%

Jordan 23%

India & Pakistan 4%

Egypt & Sudan 17%

Other Asian countries 3%

Saudi Arabia 773,000 foreign workers

N&S Yemen 43%

Oman 2%

A long journey to work

Many workers, particularly from developing countries, travel long distances to find work. In the last 15 years or so the nations of the Arabian Peninsula have attracted workers from far and wide. Almost half of the work-force in Saudi Arabia, for example, in the late 1970s were from abroad, the majority of them from developing countries, employed in construction work, hotels and other services.

Workers earn two or three times the salary they would at home, stay for a few years and send back much of their earnings to their families. For some countries their overseas workers represent an important exportable "resource". It is estimated that Pakistan, for example, has about 10 percent of its work-force employed in the Arab world, earning valuable foreign currency.

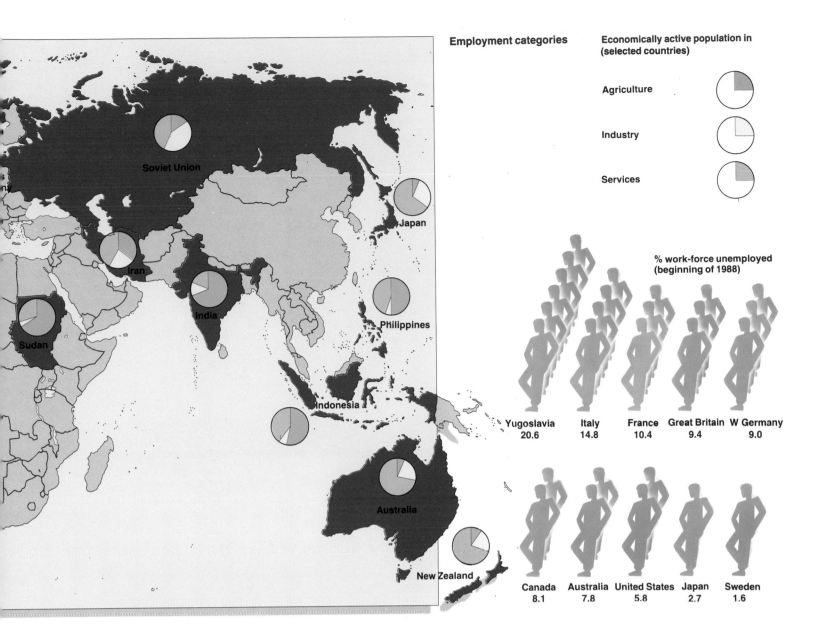

Employment categories

Economically active population in (selected countries)

Agriculture

Industry

Services

% work-force unemployed (beginning of 1988)

Yugoslavia	Italy	France	Great Britain	W Germany
20.6	14.8	10.4	9.4	9.0

Canada	Australia	United States	Japan	Sweden
8.1	7.8	5.8	2.7	1.6

Unemployment

Unemployment is not new, but in some developed countries it seems to be getting worse. The replacement of people by machines in many jobs is one cause and the production of some goods by other nations also makes some industries uncompetitive so that they have to put people out of work. The policies of government are also important.

Third World employment

Figures for the numbers of people employed and unemployed in developing countries are often difficult to get hold of and not always reliable. Many people in Third World cities work in what is called the "informal service sector", working in a small group or on their own as traders, as tailors, in small garages and repair shops, as shoe shiners and many other similar services.

19 What is Development?

The countries of western Europe and North America, with Japan, Australia and New Zealand are often referred to as 'developed' These are industrialised and urbanised countries with high material standards of living. At the other end of the scale, countries such as Bangladesh, Chad, Ethiopia and Nepal, and many others, are often said to be 'underdeveloped', 'less developed' or 'developing'.

Although there are clear differences between developed and developing nations, there are no countries that are completely developed and no nation is totally underdeveloped. In order to divide different levels of development a number of common indicators are often used, but even so not everyone would draw the dividing lines in the same place.

The map shows the classification used by The World Bank, an international organisation that monitors development and helps countries with various projects. Throughout this book various indications of development levels in different countries have been shown. See, for example, the different levels of urbanization in PEOPLE AND PLACES, the measure of health care in HEALTHY AND WEALTHY, energy production in different countries in ENERGY, the types of employment in various nations in A JOB OF WORK, and the number of telephones per 1000 population in MEDIA AND COMMUNICATIONS.

Richest and poorest

One measure used to assess development is Gross National Product (GNP). The GNP of a country is the total value of goods and services it produces in one year, and the GNP per capita (or per person) is a rough measure of the average individual income, although obviously differences exist within a country. One problem with using GNP is that Communist countries (the Soviet Union and her allies) do not issue such figures.

As an indicator of development, GNP is not perfect. Although the United Arab Emirates and Kuwait are among the five richest countries in the world they are not as developed as many European nations by other measures (see health care in HEALTHY AND WEALTHY, telephones per 1000 population in MEDIA AND COMMUNICATIONS).

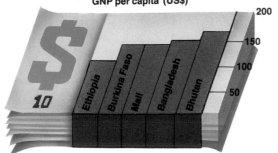

GNP per capita (US$)

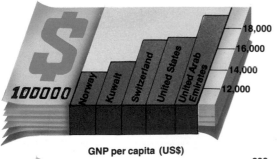

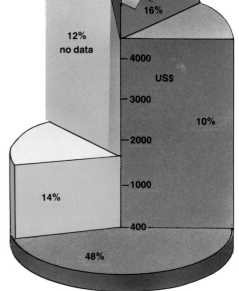

Division of wealth

How the world's population is divided according to the GNP per capita of the country in which they live. Nearly half the world population live in nations where per capita income is less than US$400.

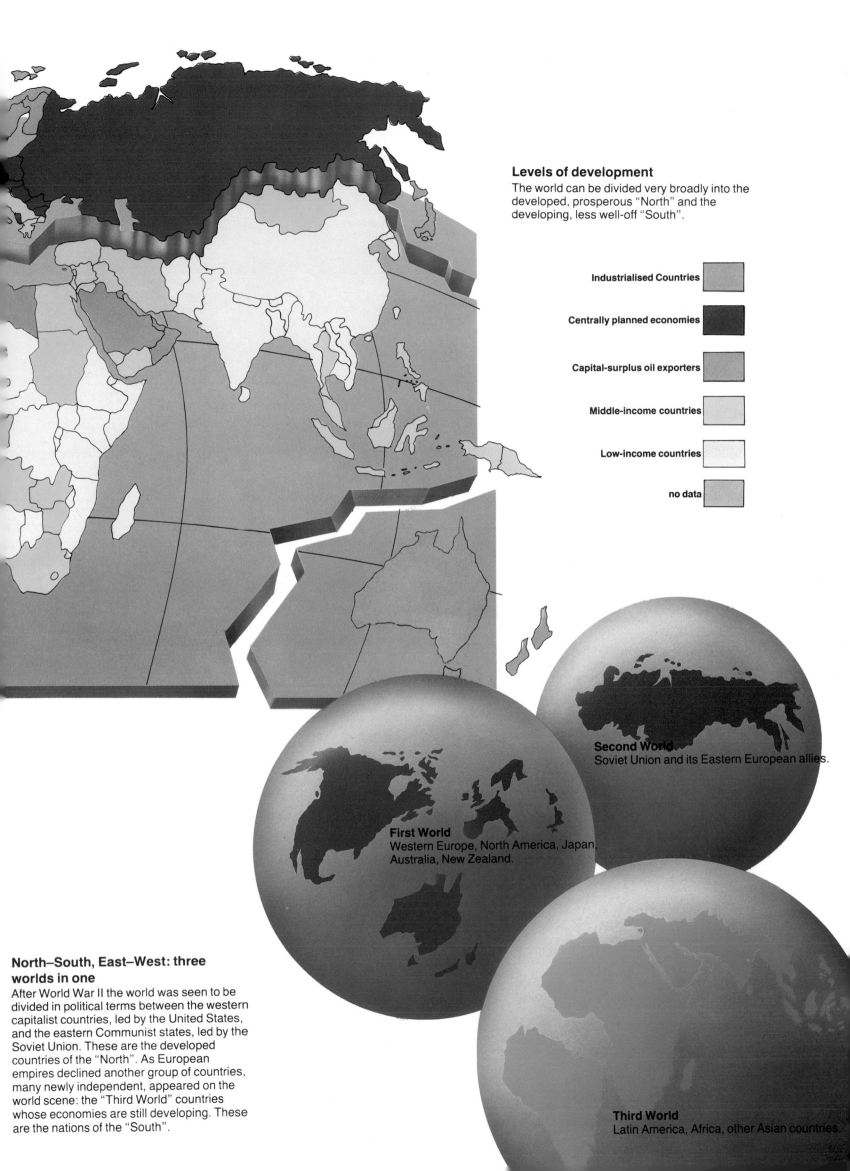

Levels of development

The world can be divided very broadly into the developed, prosperous "North" and the developing, less well-off "South".

Industrialised Countries

Centrally planned economies

Capital-surplus oil exporters

Middle-income countries

Low-income countries

no data

Second World
Soviet Union and its Eastern European allies.

First World
Western Europe, North America, Japan, Australia, New Zealand.

Third World
Latin America, Africa, other Asian countries.

North–South, East–West: three worlds in one

After World War II the world was seen to be divided in political terms between the western capitalist countries, led by the United States, and the eastern Communist states, led by the Soviet Union. These are the developed countries of the "North". As European empires declined another group of countries, many newly independent, appeared on the world scene: the "Third World" countries whose economies are still developing. These are the nations of the "South".

20 Foreign Aid

Foreign aid covers many different arrangements for the world's rich countries giving money and help to the poorer nations. Few of these arrangements, however, are simply gifts. Usually foreign aid involves the receiving countries promising to use the money to buy equipment, goods or services from the donor country. Even when developed countries give emergency food aid it is sometimes a good way to dispose of food that they have produced too much of.

There are three main groups of countries that give foreign aid. These are the Western nations of the Organisation for Economic Cooperation and Development (OECD), the Communist countries of the Soviet bloc, and the big oil-producing members of the Organisation of Petroleum Exporting Countries (OPEC). Some nations receive aid and also give it. Saudi Arabia and Venezuela, for example, receive aid in return for cheap oil.

Some of the foreign aid given is 'bilateral aid', which means a private arrangement between one giving and one receiving country. The other main category of aid is that given to international organisations such as the United Nations (UN) agencies. In addition to government aid, there is also a large contribution made by private charities.

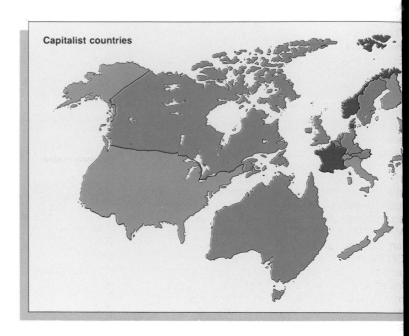

Capitalist countries

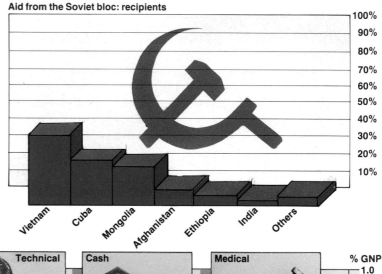

Aid from the Soviet bloc: recipients

100%
90%
80%
70%
60%
50%
40%
30%
20%
10%

Vietnam Cuba Mongolia Afghanistan Ethiopia India Others

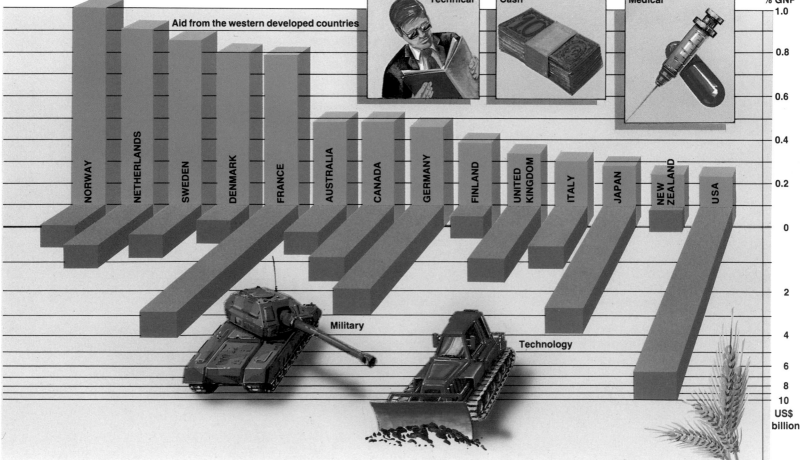

Aid from the western developed countries

Technical   Cash   Medical

% GNP
1.0
0.8
0.6
0.4
0.2
0

NORWAY NETHERLANDS SWEDEN DENMARK FRANCE AUSTRALIA CANADA GERMANY FINLAND UNITED KINGDOM ITALY JAPAN NEW ZEALAND USA

Military

Technology

2
4
6
8
10
US$ billion

Food

Aid from the Soviet Bloc

The richer countries of the Council for Mutual Economic Assistance (CMEA) give to the poorer Communist countries and others. The emphasis of aid to Vietnam, whose economy was devastated in the war of the late 1960s and early 1970s, is on power stations, infrastructure, fuel industries and agricultural irrigation. In Mongolia, the third largest receiver of CMEA aid and second largest receiver of aid from the Soviet Union, money is put into the development of mining and agriculture, particularly animal husbandry. Many citizens from these countries are also trained and educated in the Soviet Union and other eastern European countries.

Aid from the Western developed countries

The United States is the largest aid donor, but the United States is a very rich country. When a country's aid is measured as a proportion of its total national income (GNP) Norway is the most generous of these nations. Some of the OPEC countries give more than 2 per cent of their national income.

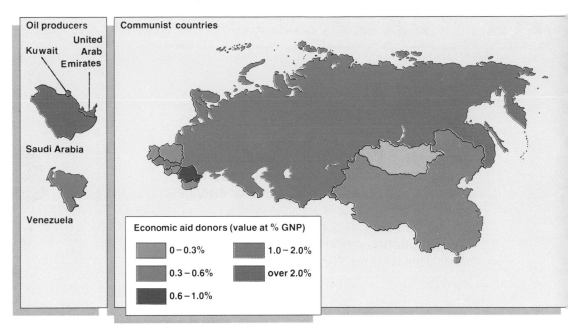

Oil producers

Kuwait United Arab Emirates

Saudi Arabia

Venezuela

Communist countries

Economic aid donors (value at % GNP)

0 – 0.3%	1.0 – 2.0%
0.3 – 0.6%	over 2.0%
0.6 – 1.0%	

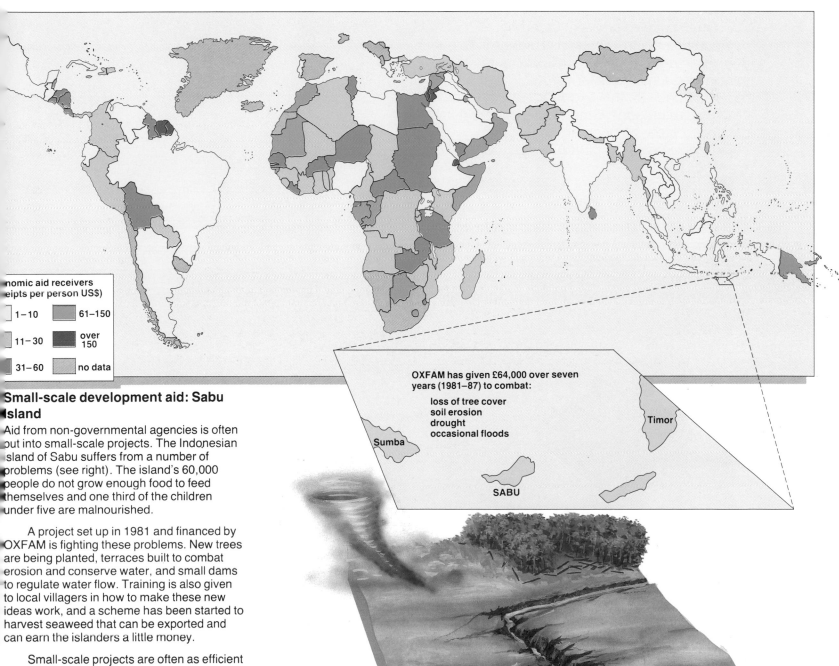

Economic aid receivers (receipts per person US$)

1–10	61–150
11–30	over 150
31–60	no data

OXFAM has given £64,000 over seven years (1981–87) to combat:

loss of tree cover
soil erosion
drought
occasional floods

Sumba

SABU

Timor

Small-scale development aid: Sabu Island

Aid from non-governmental agencies is often put into small-scale projects. The Indonesian island of Sabu suffers from a number of problems (see right). The island's 60,000 people do not grow enough food to feed themselves and one third of the children under five are malnourished.

A project set up in 1981 and financed by OXFAM is fighting these problems. New trees are being planted, terraces built to combat erosion and conserve water, and small dams to regulate water flow. Training is also given to local villagers in how to make these new ideas work, and a scheme has been started to harvest seaweed that can be exported and can earn the islanders a little money.

Small-scale projects are often as efficient a way of spending aid money as the building of large, impressive schemes such as dams. The small-scale approach helps local people to develop their skills using quite simple methods.

45

21 Trade

Trade is important to every country. Each can sell goods and materials it produces and with the money buy products that it needs from other nations. Generally, the larger the country the smaller its role in international trade in proportion to its size, since larger countries usually have more of their own resources. In the United States, for example, the value of imports and exports is for each less than 10 per cent of the country's GNP. The Netherlands' imports and exports, however, both approach 50 per cent of its GNP. Even so, the United States is still the world's greatest trading nation, since it has such a large GNP.

One common problem faced by developing countries in world trade is that they often rely heavily on just one major export (see Oman's reliance on oil, right). If the world price for this export is high the country can prosper, Oman has become rich on its oil. Often the price of Third World commodities such as coffee, sugar, copper or tin varies greatly from year to year so that the producing country cannot rely on a stable income from its main export.

There have been many attempts to unite Third World primary producers, so that prices for their commodities can be made stable, but apart from the success of producers in controlling oil prices, most of these attempts have failed.

Pattern of trade: United States

The United States' main trading partners are its northern and southern neighbours (Canada and Mexico), Japan and the United Kingdom. Compared to Oman, for example, the United States has more trading partners and is not as heavily dependent on just one or two.

The things that the United States exports are also more diverse, which is more healthy for its economy. One problem the US does have is that throughout the 1980s it has been importing much more, by value, than it has been exporting. This "trade deficit" puts strains on the US economy.

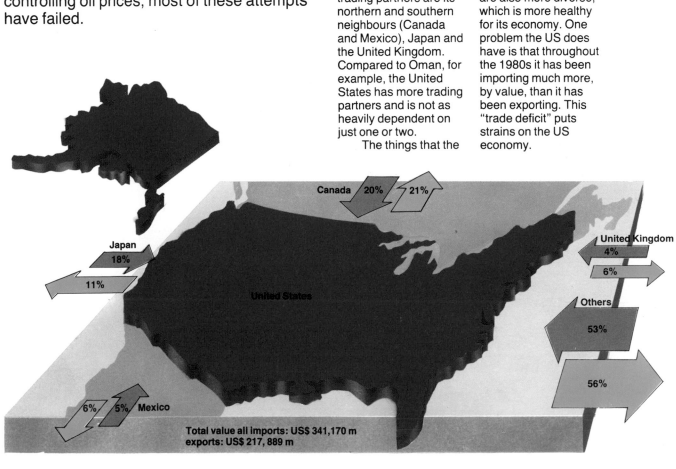

Canada 20% 21%

Japan 18%

11%

United States

United Kingdom 4%

6%

Others 53%

56%

6% 5% Mexico

Total value all imports: US$ 341,170 m
exports: US$ 217,889 m

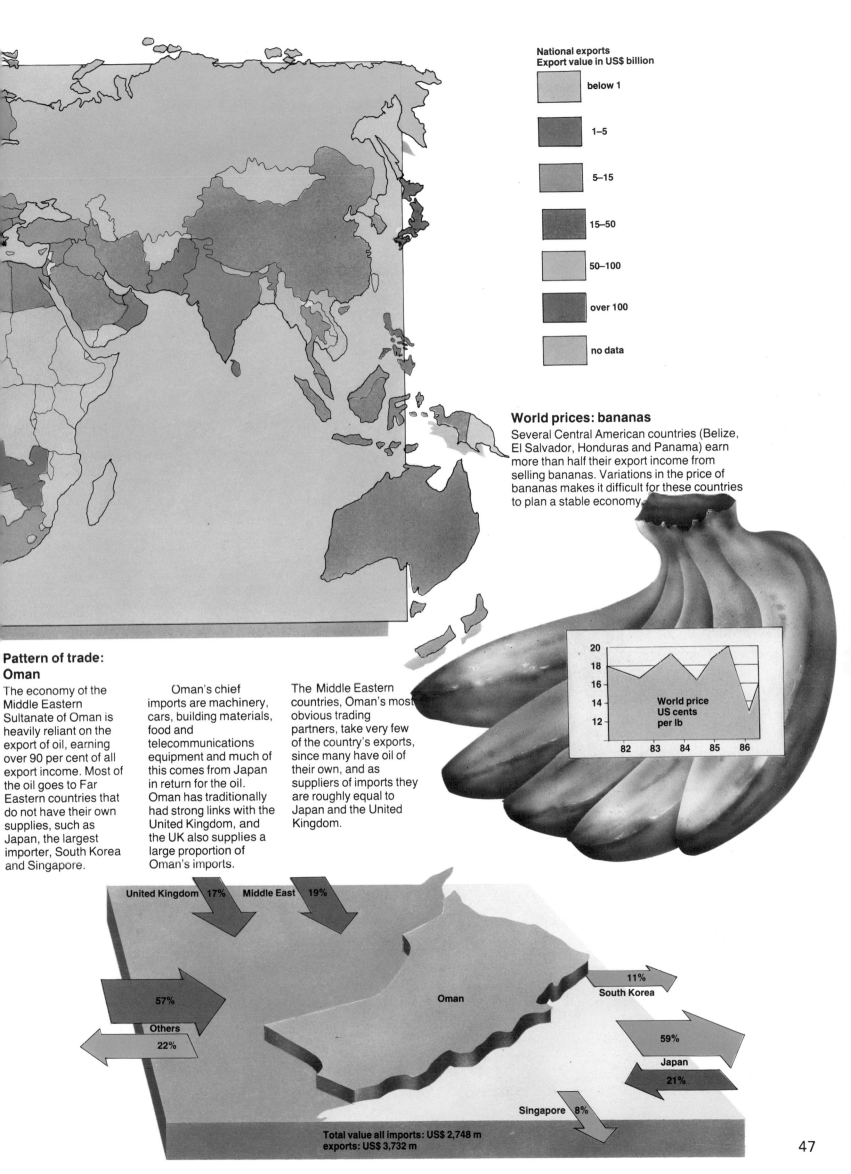

National exports
Export value in US$ billion

below 1

1–5

5–15

15–50

50–100

over 100

no data

World prices: bananas

Several Central American countries (Belize, El Salvador, Honduras and Panama) earn more than half their export income from selling bananas. Variations in the price of bananas makes it difficult for these countries to plan a stable economy.

World price
US cents
per lb

20
18
16
14
12

82 83 84 85 86

Pattern of trade: Oman

The economy of the Middle Eastern Sultanate of Oman is heavily reliant on the export of oil, earning over 90 per cent of all export income. Most of the oil goes to Far Eastern countries that do not have their own supplies, such as Japan, the largest importer, South Korea and Singapore.

Oman's chief imports are machinery, cars, building materials, food and telecommunications equipment and much of this comes from Japan in return for the oil. Oman has traditionally had strong links with the United Kingdom, and the UK also supplies a large proportion of Oman's imports.

The Middle Eastern countries, Oman's most obvious trading partners, take very few of the country's exports, since many have oil of their own, and as suppliers of imports they are roughly equal to Japan and the United Kingdom.

United Kingdom 17% Middle East 19%

57%

Others
22%

Oman

11%
South Korea

59%
Japan
21%

Singapore 8%

Total value all imports: US$ 2,748 m
exports: US$ 3,732 m

22 Tourism & Leisure

International tourism has expanded dramatically in the last 30 years or so, and the large majority of tourists come from the developed countries. It is easy to understand why so many people in Western Europe, for example, often travel to foreign countries. Travel is fast and the countries are relatively small and close together. The citizens of these nations are also rich and can afford to have holidays abroad. In Europe the largest tourist movement is towards the sun, from the cool north to the warm south.

The money tourists spend is a useful source of income for the countries they visit. The Communist states welcome tourists from the west because they bring much-needed 'hard currency', but at the same time their movements are closely controlled.

For poorer countries too the money is welcome, and there are many opportunities for jobs in hotels and selling and making souvenirs. The North African country of Tunisia, for example, has developed its tourist industry in the last ten years to attract Europeans in search of the sun. Tourists do not just bring benefits however (see below), the season is often short so that employment is usually for just part of the year and tourist destinations may go out of fashion.

Impact on a small developing count
Antigua

Antigua is one of the small developing Caribbean islands that have become leadin destinations for tourists from the richer nations. The tourist industry has created ov 2,000 jobs in Antigua and its neighbouring island of Barbuda, which together have a population of some 80,000. Tourism also accounts for about one fifth of the country's Gross Domestic Product.

There are also some problems caused by the development of tourism. Jobs are seasonal, and the number of tourists varies from year to year, 1975 and 1976 for example, were bad years all over the Caribbean (see left). Many of the hotels in Antigua are owned by foreign companies, s that profits leave the country. Also, although the hotels buy sea food from local fishermer most of the other foods are imported rather than bought in the local markets. Tourism ca also make local people resentful when they see rich visitors living in a better style than they themselves can afford.

Tourist arrivals

Jobs

2,600

1,600

(low season)   (high season)

100,000

50,000

0

1960   1965   1970   1975   1980 1982

Antigua

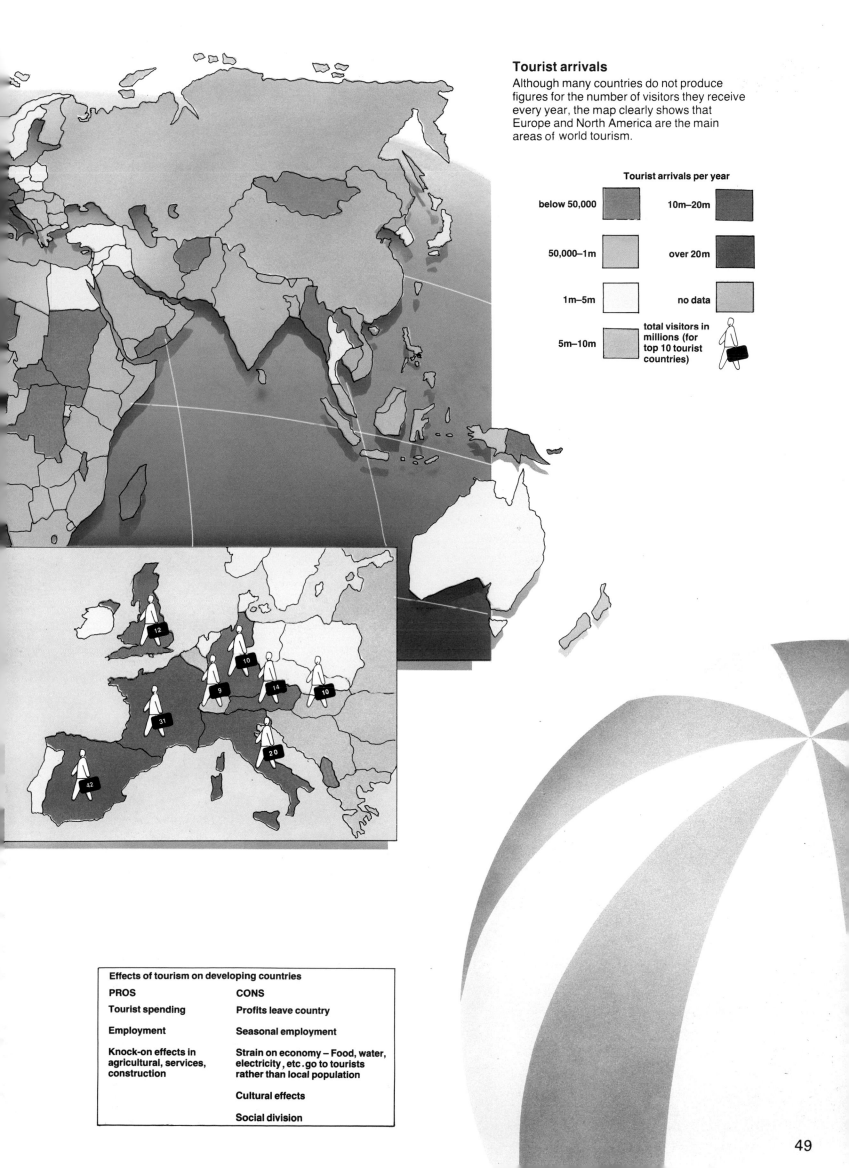

Tourist arrivals

Although many countries do not produce figures for the number of visitors they receive every year, the map clearly shows that Europe and North America are the main areas of world tourism.

Tourist arrivals per year

below 50,000	10m–20m
50,000–1m	over 20m
1m–5m	no data
5m–10m	total visitors in millions (for top 10 tourist countries)

Effects of tourism on developing countries	
PROS	**CONS**
Tourist spending	Profits leave country
Employment	Seasonal employment
Knock-on effects in agricultural, services, construction	Strain on economy – Food, water, electricity, etc. go to tourists rather than local population
	Cultural effects
	Social division

23 Transport

People in the rich countries are generally more mobile than those in poorer nations. As the map shows, the number of cars and buses as a proportion of population is greated in North America, western Europe, Australia and New Zealand. In many African countries motor vehicles are numerous in the big cities, but in rural areas they are few and far between. Farmers in such countries cannot afford their own cars, they would have little use for them anyway, and there are few roads.

Air travel, also dominantly a rich country's form of transport, has grown very rapidly since World War II. International transport of people and cargo is much faster by air than by sea. Although since World War II the world's merchant shipping fleets have grown by about five times in terms of tonnage, the actual number of ships has increased very little in this period. Ships have merely grown larger, oil tankers being the most obvious example of this trend.

Rail traffic in the developed world has generally decreased in recent years, with road transport becoming more important. In the Soviet Union and other eastern European countries, however, and many Third World countries, the railways are still of greater importance, especially for moving goods.

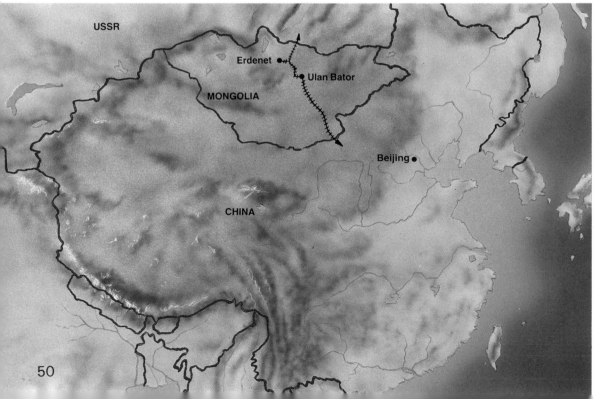

Trans-Mongolian railway: an economic lifeline

As recently as the 1920s, the Central Asian Republic of Mongolia was in a very backward state of development. Since then the country has raced forward to become a middle-income country (see WHAT IS DEVELOPMENT?), with much foreign aid from the Soviet Union. A key factor in this development was the construction of the railway, completed in 1956. The railway is used to transport Mongolia's exports (animal products and metals) and bring in much-needed machinery, food and equipment.

Building the railway was not easy: in southern Mongolia it passes through the Gobi Desert and in the north the ground is unstable because it becomes frozen in the winter and marshy in summer.

Many other "land-locked" countries (those without a sea coast) also depend heavily on railways for communication with the outside world. They include Bolivia in South America and Zambia in Africa.

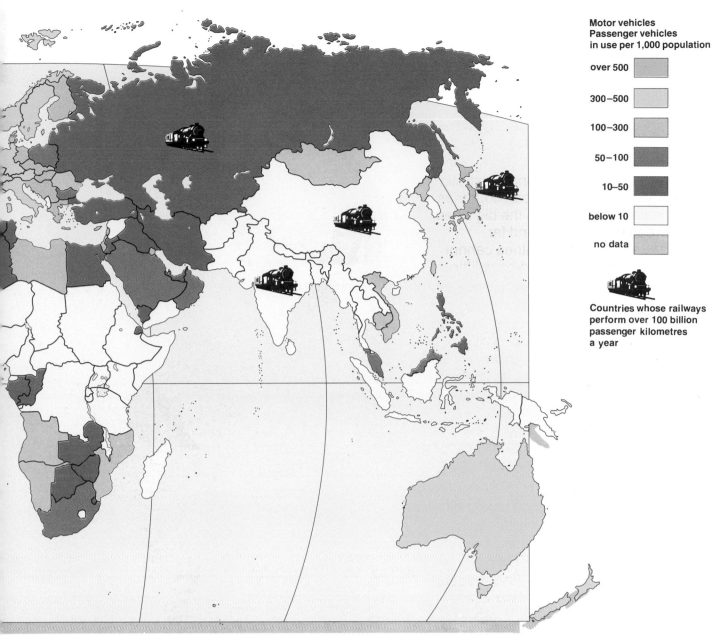

Motor vehicles
Passenger vehicles
in use per 1,000 population

over 500

300–500

100–300

50–100

10–50

below 10

no data

Countries whose railways
perform over 100 billion
passenger kilometres
a year

Cars on the road

In some countries, particularly small rich
states, if every car took to the road at once the
entire system would probably come to a halt.
In Hong Kong there is one vehicle for every
4.1 metres of road. In larger countries road
congestion is typical of the big cities. The
traffic chaos in Lagos, Nigeria is so bad that a
law has been passed only allowing cars with
even-numbered licence plates to be driven on
Mondays, Wednesdays and Fridays, and odd
numbers of Tuesdays, Thursday and
Saturdays. For those who can afford it
however, they simply have two cars, one
even-numbered, one odd.

Air travel

By far the largest carriers of air passengers
are the airlines of the United States, who flew
over 500 billion passenger-kilometres in
1985. Most of these passengers were
travelling within the United States. The Soviet
Union's national airline, Aeroflot, also carries
most if its passengers on domestic flights,
whereas the other countries shown, most of
them much smaller, carried the majority of
their passengers on international flights.

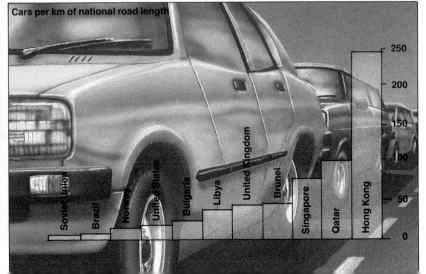

Cars per km of national road length

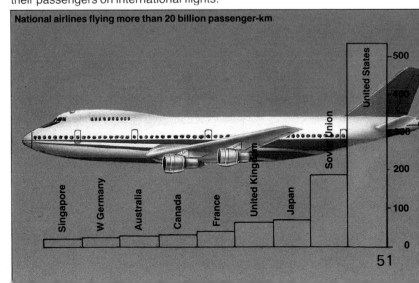

National airlines flying more than 20 billion passenger-km

During the 20th century the world has experienced a 'communications revolution'. With radio, television and telephone, international communication has been made fast and easy, using satellites, undersea cables and computers. The same technology makes news travel fast, so that newspapers can tell us about the current events around the world within minutes or hours of the important happenings.

Many of these forms of communication are more numerous in the rich, developed countries. For example, while the people of the United States have on average 80 telephones per hundred population, in China they have less than one. Likewise, in North America and more recently in Europe satellites are increasing the choice of television channels for the viewer, while in many other countries there is just a handful of stations often run by national governments.

Radios have been a useful tool in the development of many Third World countries, bringing education and news to rural populations. Radios are fairly cheap, can be listened to by many people, and have an advantage over printed books and newspapers in that they can be understood by those who cannot read. Since the audiences for radio broadcasts are so large, many countries have radio services especially for those listeners abroad (see far right).

Communications revolution

Advances in computer and satellite technology have made the communications revolution of the 20th century possible. Computers allow us to keep large quantities of information and control complicated systems such as telephone networks. Satellites can be used to transmit information fast around the world, as well as to collect information on the weather and many other natural and human events across the globe. There are about 300 satellites operating in orbit over the earth.

Circulation of daily newspapers per 1000 population

Telephones

Number of telephones per thousand population. Telephone calls are made using cables above the ground, under the ground or on the ocean bed, and satellites.

Brazil 48

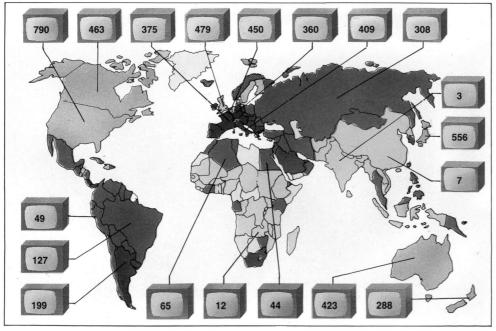

| 790 | 463 | 375 | 479 | 450 | 360 | 409 | 308 |

3

556

7

49

127

199

65

12

44

423

288

▢	0–10
▣	11–100
▪	101–250
▨	251–500
▧	501–850

Telephones in use per 1000 inhabitants

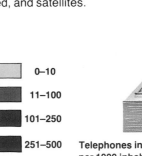

Television receivers per 1000 inhabitants

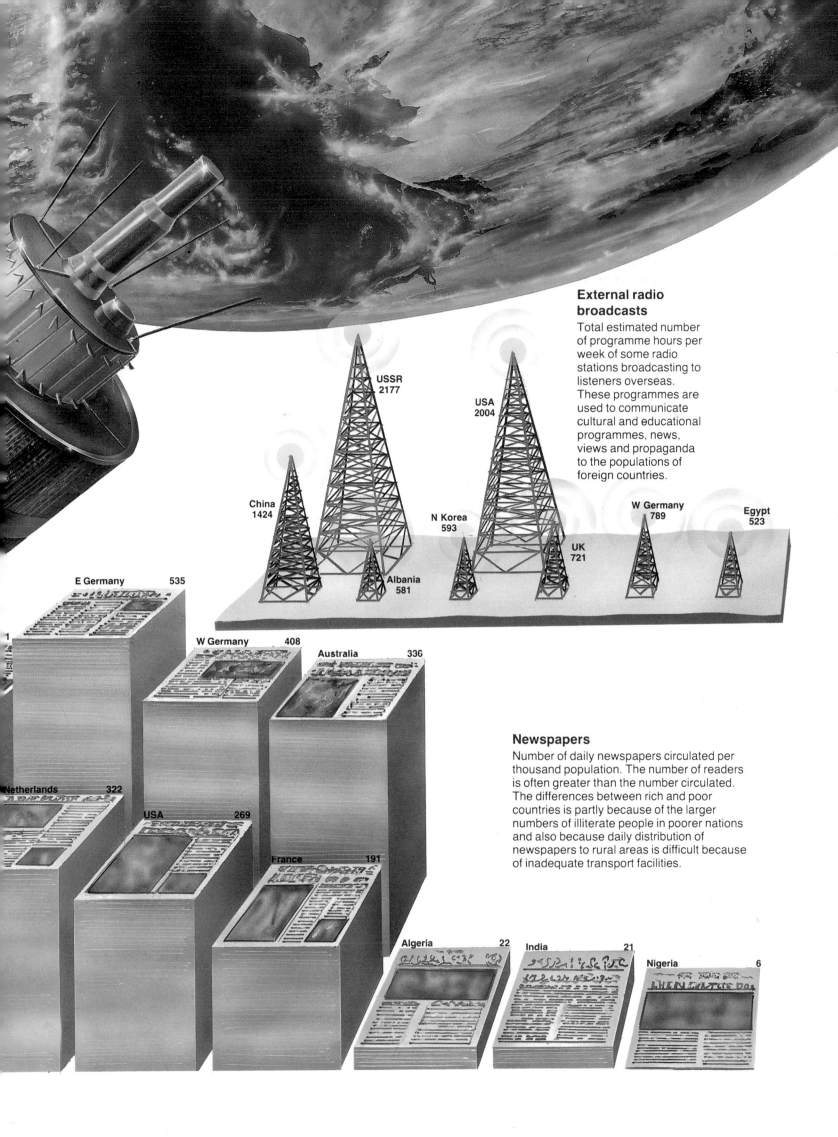

External radio broadcasts

Total estimated number of programme hours per week of some radio stations broadcasting to listeners overseas. These programmes are used to communicate cultural and educational programmes, news, views and propaganda to the populations of foreign countries.

USSR 2177
USA 2004
China 1424
N Korea 593
Albania 581
UK 721
W Germany 789
Egypt 523

E Germany 535
W Germany 408
Australia 336
Netherlands 322
USA 269
France 191

Newspapers

Number of daily newspapers circulated per thousand population. The number of readers is often greater than the number circulated. The differences between rich and poor countries is partly because of the larger numbers of illiterate people in poorer nations and also because daily distribution of newspapers to rural areas is difficult because of inadequate transport facilities.

Algeria 22
India 21
Nigeria 6

25 Language, Religion & Culture

The language a people speak, their religion and their culture are all closely related. For example, many Muslims, members of the Islamic faith, are part of the Arab world that is spread from Mauritania in West Africa, across North Africa and the Middle East to Pakistan. Most Muslims speak a common language: Arabic. At the same time, many people in the North African countries of Morocco, Algeria and Tunisia also speak French since they were once part of the French Empire.

In Latin America, from Mexico to Argentina, the dominant religion is Roman Catholicism, and most people speak Spanish. This religion and language was brought by the Spanish who ruled this area for 200–300 years from the 16th century. In many parts of Latin America there are also native Indians who have their own languages and cultures that go back to before the Spanish conquest.

The Communist countries of the world do not officially allow religious practices, but many continue to worship in secret.

Throughout history conquering and ruling peoples have tried to change native language, religion and culture. In China during the 1960s and 1970s a 'Cultural Revolution' occurred, which involved sweeping and often violent changes in all parts of Chinese life.

World's principal languages

Nearly 40 per cent of the world's population (about 1,800 million people) speak just five languages. Whereas most Guoyo speakers live in China, English is widely spoken in Australia, Bahamas, Canada, Cyprus, Eire, Gambia, Ghana, Guyana, India, Jamaica, Kenya, Malaysia, Malta, New Zealand, Nigeria, Pakistan, Sierra Leone, Singapore, South Africa, Sri Lanka, Tanzania, Trinidad and Tobago, Uganda, UK, USA and Zimbabwe.

Guoyo (Standard Northern Chinese)

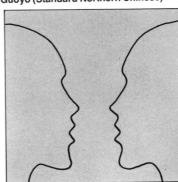

English

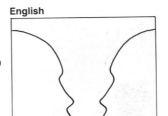

Russian

Hindustani

Spanish

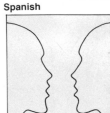

1% of world's population

Muslim   **Roman Catholic**

World population by religion
1 figure = 1% of world population

Shinto   Taoist

Jewish

Eastern Orthodox   Confucian   Buddhist   Protestant   Hindu

Power of religion

The influence of religion over people, and thereby the power of some religious leaders, cannot be denied. In Iran, for example, the head of government is a religious leader: the Ayatollah Khomeini (see GOVERNMENT). The revolution that brought the Ayatollah's government to power in 1979 occurred in response to the Shah's efforts to change Iranian culture. The Shah tried to introduce Iran to western European culture, but the speed of change provoked a national uprising.

In Iran today the traditional values of Islam have been re-introduced. Thus, for example, women must wear veils in the streets and play a secondary role to men, while the power of the religious leaders has been brought back to the fore.

Eight great religions

RELIGION	MAIN AREAS	WHEN IT BEGAN	FOUNDER
HINDUISM	India	Before 2000 BC	No specific founder
JUDAISM	USA, Israel, USSR	Before 1200 BC	Abraham
SHINTO	Japan	By 600 BC	No specific founder
TAOISM	China	By 500 BC	Lao-tzu
BUDDHISM	Far East and South East Asia	About 500 BC	Siddhartha Gautama
CHRISTIANITY	Europe, North and South America	After AD 4	Jesus Christ
ISLAM	From West Africa to Indonesia	AD 622	Muhammad
SIKHISM	Punjab (India)	About AD 1500	Guru Nanak

Languages of the world

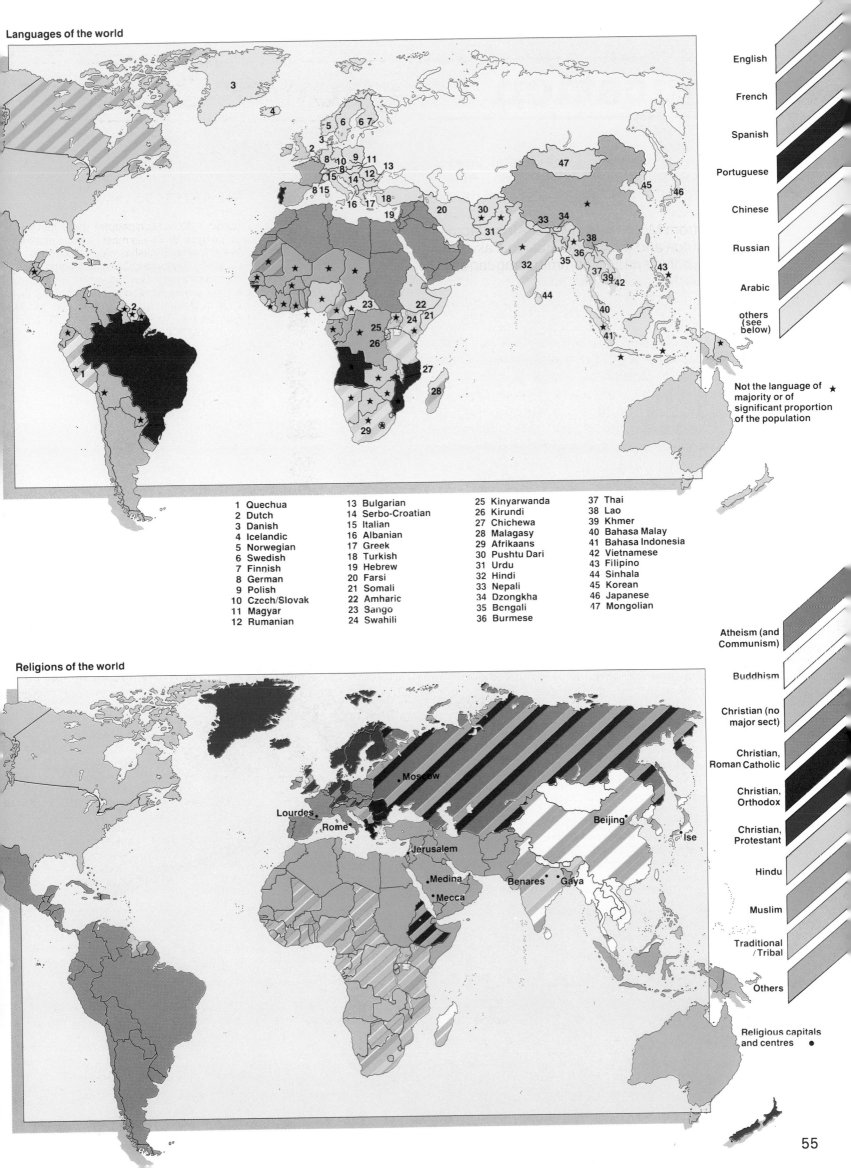

English	
French	
Spanish	
Portuguese	
Chinese	
Russian	
Arabic	
others (see below)	

Not the language of majority or of significant proportion of the population ★

1 Quechua
2 Dutch
3 Danish
4 Icelandic
5 Norwegian
6 Swedish
7 Finnish
8 German
9 Polish
10 Czech/Slovak
11 Magyar
12 Rumanian

13 Bulgarian
14 Serbo-Croatian
15 Italian
16 Albanian
17 Greek
18 Turkish
19 Hebrew
20 Farsi
21 Somali
22 Amharic
23 Sango
24 Swahili

25 Kinyarwanda
26 Kirundi
27 Chichewa
28 Malagasy
29 Afrikaans
30 Pushtu Dari
31 Urdu
32 Hindi
33 Nepali
34 Dzongkha
35 Bengali
36 Burmese

37 Thai
38 Lao
39 Khmer
40 Bahasa Malay
41 Bahasa Indonesia
42 Vietnamese
43 Filipino
44 Sinhala
45 Korean
46 Japanese
47 Mongolian

Religions of the world

Atheism (and Communism)	
Buddhism	
Christian (no major sect)	
Christian, Roman Catholic	
Christian, Orthodox	
Christian, Protestant	
Hindu	
Muslim	
Traditional /Tribal	
Others	

Religious capitals and centres ●

55

26 Education

Education is important, since children need to learn in order to become responsible adults. The information on the map measures rates of 'formal education', or learning in the class room. Just as important as this is the knowledge and wisdom gained from experience of living in the world, but this is much harder to measure.

The map shows that particularly in Africa there are many countries where more than half of the children do not even receive primary education. Often this is simply because there are no schools. It is not surprising then to note that the majority of adults in these countries are illiterate (they cannot read or write). In most countries men are, on average, more literate than women.

A certain number of years of formal education is compulsory in almost every nation, but this is often not enforced because perhaps there are no schools or teachers, or at certain times of the year, such as harvest time, schoolboys and girls are needed to help in the fields.

Education spending

The annual amount spent by a selection of governments on education of all kinds as a proportion of the national GNP.

Pupils per teacher

The number of pupils that the average teacher has to teach in his or her class, the "pupil/teacher ratio", varies enormously from country to country. It follows that children in a class of 20 will get more attention from a teacher than pupils in a class of 50. Thus, the smaller the pupil/teacher ratio the better it is for a child's education.

Educational expenditure as % GNP

USA · UK · France · W Germany · Netherlands · India · Australia · Peru · Libya

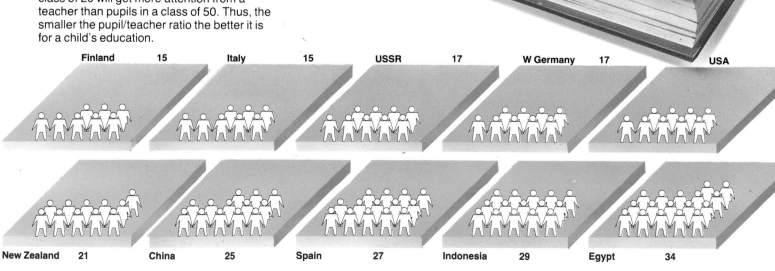

| Finland | 15 | Italy | 15 | USSR | 17 | W Germany | 17 | USA | |
| New Zealand | 21 | China | 25 | Spain | 27 | Indonesia | 29 | Egypt | 34 |

Pupil/Teacher ratios

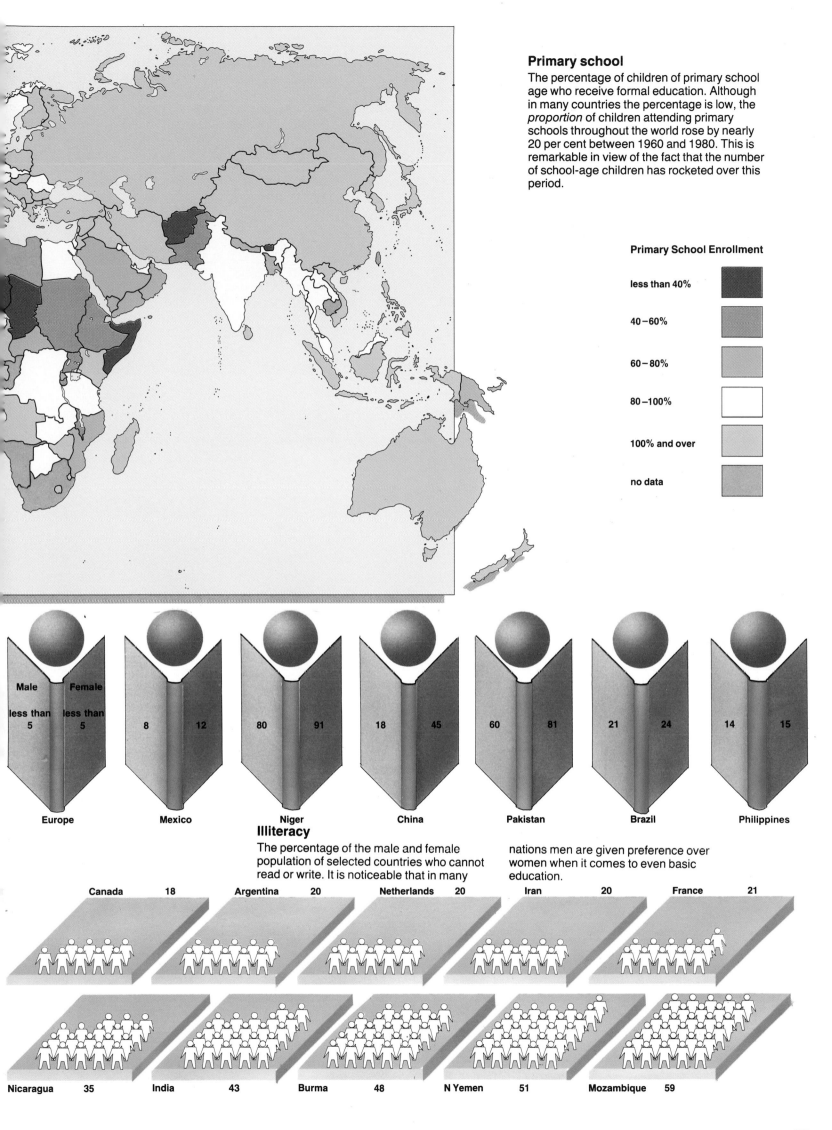

Primary school

The percentage of children of primary school age who receive formal education. Although in many countries the percentage is low, the *proportion* of children attending primary schools throughout the world rose by nearly 20 per cent between 1960 and 1980. This is remarkable in view of the fact that the number of school-age children has rocketed over this period.

Primary School Enrollment

less than 40%

40–60%

60–80%

80–100%

100% and over

no data

	Male	Female
Europe	less than 5	less than 5
Mexico	8	12
Niger	80	91
China	18	45
Pakistan	60	81
Brazil	21	24
Philippines	14	15

Illiteracy

The percentage of the male and female population of selected countries who cannot read or write. It is noticeable that in many nations men are given preference over women when it comes to even basic education.

Canada	18	Argentina	20	Netherlands	20	Iran	20	France	21
Nicaragua	35	India	43	Burma	48	N Yemen	51	Mozambique	59

57

27 Government

Governments run nations. In this country the government is 'democratically elected', which means that all adults have a free choice to vote from a selection of political parties and their candidates. The government is then formed by the party that gains a majority of the votes in the general elections that are held every few years.

No system of government is perfect, but in western and some other countries most people agree that this form of democracy is the best that has been thought of. At the same time, anyone is free to say and think what they like, including disagreeing with the government. In doing so they are protected by the law. Most of the time, but not always, this system works well.

Many other countries have different types of government (see map). In Communist states people can vote in elections but usually the candidates are all from the same party. Thus, the government is always run by the same (the only) party. 'Freedom of speech' is also more limited in such states.

In South Africa the country is ruled by a minority of white people who vote for their government. In many other African countries which have only been independent for a short time (see NATIONS), there is fighting between groups to gain control of their country (see map below and main map).

■ Communist states, elections but no free choice	□ Democratic elections & choice of parties but limitations favouring an elite
■ One party states, government largely autocratic	■ Autocratic governments with or without some popular representation
■ Democratic elections with choice of parties	■ No government control over substantial area

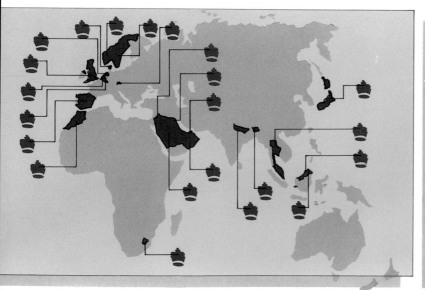

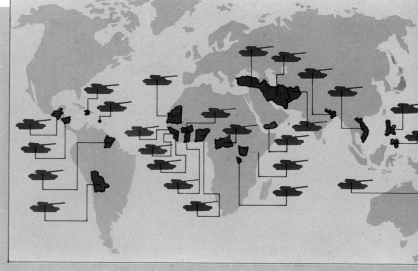

Monarchies
A monarch is a supreme ruler over a country, with a title such as king, queen, emperor or sultan. In European countries kings and queens now have little power however, but in other nations such as Saudi Arabia the king is head of government.

Governments at risk
Countries whose governments have been overthrown by force during the 1980s. A comparison of this map with the main map in NATIONS shows that it is largely the countries that have become independent since World War II that suffer from such forceful overthrow of governments.

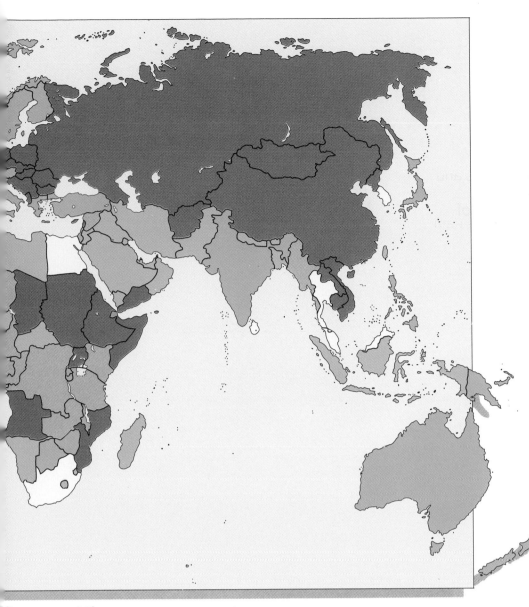

Governments in power

Although no two governments are exactly similar, this map shows a broad division of the powers that rule the world today. An example of the type of government in each division is given below.

Communist states: USSR

Since the revolution of 1917 the Communist Party has ruled the Soviet Union. As there are no other official political parties only the Communist Party can effectively form a government to rule the country.

Democratic states: UK

The Prime Minister, Mrs Margaret Thatcher, was elected democratically in 1987, against three main opposition parties. Elections must be held at least every five years, but they can be held earlier if the government chooses.

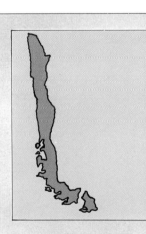

One party states: Chile

The current Head of State, General Pinochet, came to power after the government was overthrown in a *coup d'etat* in 1973. Political opposition is restricted and there have been no elections since the coup.

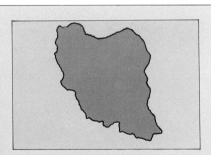

Autocratic states: Iran

The present government of Iran is headed by a religious leader: the Ayatollah Khomeini. Khomeini came to power in the "Islamic Revolution" of 1979, deposing the Shah, a sort of monarch. Khomeini's government has some popular support, although information on political feelings within Iran is hard to come by.

Democratic states with elites: Mexico

Although Mexico holds regular elections, the most powerful party, the Partido Revolucionario Institucional or PRI, has not lost an election since the present constitution was made in 1917. The government has often been accused of fixing the election results.

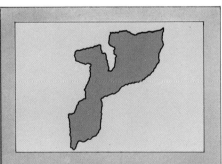

No government control: Mozambique

Mozambique has a Communist government, but large parts of the country are controlled by guerilla forces fighting against the government. In these conditions, virtually a civil war, a country is almost impossible to govern.

28 A World at War

Since 1945 many more people have been killed by bombs and bullets than the total number of military casualties of World War II. During this 40 years or so there have been more than 100 wars around the globe. The world is now dominated by two 'superpowers', the USA and the USSR, and although these countries have not met face-to-face in conflict they have been involved in many of the wars in other nations: supplying weapons, advisers and giving political support.

It is often said that the fragile peace between the superpowers is maintained by the threat of nuclear weapons that are so powerful that these countries are perhaps frightened to use them. Instead the superpowers meet indirectly, often by supporting opposing sides in Third World conflicts.

Conflicts can be divided into wars between countries, disputes over borders, wars of independence and civil wars. Civil wars were responsible for the large number of deaths in Nigeria and Bangladesh in recent times (see map). Civil conflicts and fights for independence do not always become full-scale wars, and in modern times terrorism has become widespread. A small group of revolutionaries or freedom fighters can often create immense damage and unrest.

One of the roles of the United Nations (see NATIONS) is to prevent conflict and wars, and UN peace-keeping forces have tried to help in many of the world's trouble spots.

Big spenders

These are the countries who spend the most money on defence per person of their population. In absolute terms, the USA and the USSR spend by far the most, in both cases over US$200 billion a year. It seems strange, however, that while the USA, for example, spends over US$1,000 a year protecting each citizen, many of them dare not walk the streets at night.

Defence budgets (billions of US$)

India East Germany Italy Saudi Arabia Japan West Germany France UK USA USSR

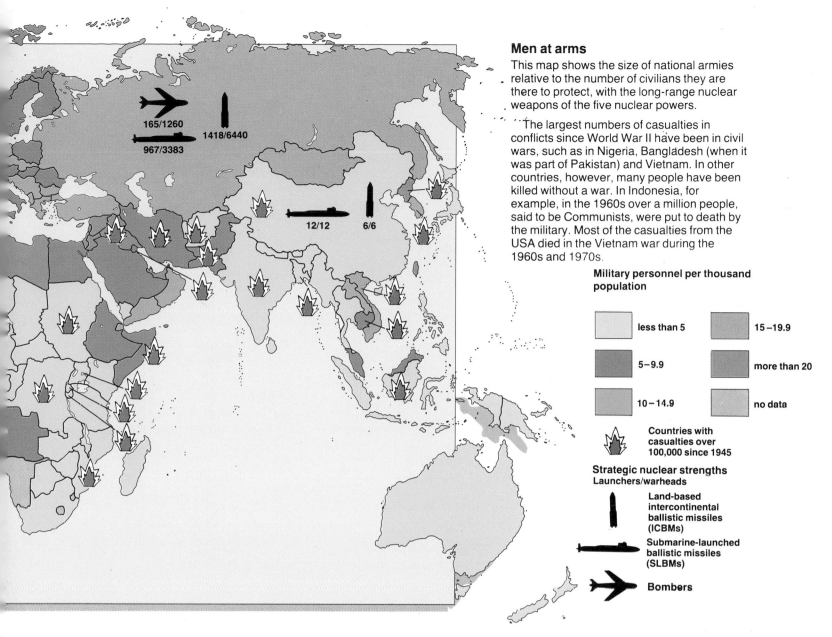

Men at arms

This map shows the size of national armies relative to the number of civilians they are there to protect, with the long-range nuclear weapons of the five nuclear powers.

The largest numbers of casualties in conflicts since World War II have been in civil wars, such as in Nigeria, Bangladesh (when it was part of Pakistan) and Vietnam. In other countries, however, many people have been killed without a war. In Indonesia, for example, in the 1960s over a million people, said to be Communists, were put to death by the military. Most of the casualties from the USA died in the Vietnam war during the 1960s and 1970s.

Military personnel per thousand population

less than 5	15–19.9
5–9.9	more than 20
10–14.9	no data

Countries with casualties over 100,000 since 1945

Strategic nuclear strengths
Launchers/warheads

Land-based intercontinental ballistic missiles (ICBMs)

Submarine-launched ballistic missiles (SLBMs)

Bombers

Military manpower

The comparative strengths of the armies of the NATO and Warsaw Pact countries (see NATIONS) and the Chinese army, which after the USSR is the world's second largest national army. The Chinese armed forces are stationed almost entirely within China, whereas the USSR and the USA have large numbers of their troops stationed in Europe, the most important strategic area between the two superpowers.

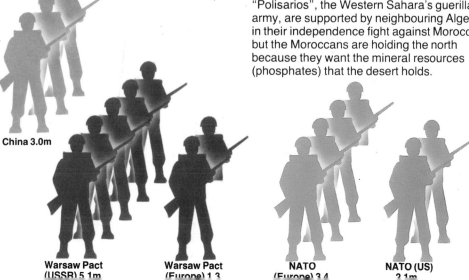

China 3.0m

Warsaw Pact (USSR) 5.1m

Warsaw Pact (Europe) 1.3

NATO (Europe) 3.4

NATO (US) 2.1m

Fighting for Independence: Western Sahara

Most African countries have become independent since World War II, after being part of European empires for many years. One nation still fighting for independence is the Western Sahara. This country on the West African coast was the Spanish Sahara until 1975, when Spain withdrew. Although the United Nations proclaimed the Western Sahara to be independent, in 1976 the country was divided between Morocco and Mauritania.

Three years later Mauritania pulled out of the country, but Morocco still occupies the northern half of the Western Sahara. The "Polisarios", the Western Sahara's guerilla army, are supported by neighbouring Algeria in their independence fight against Morocco, but the Moroccans are holding the north because they want the mineral resources (phosphates) that the desert holds.

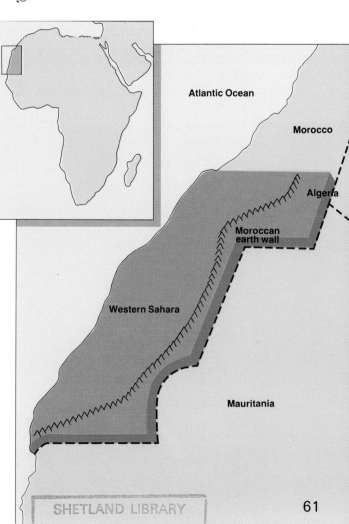

Atlantic Ocean

Morocco

Algeria

Moroccan earth wall

Western Sahara

Mauritania

Index